ANSWER TO ANXIETY

BY HERMAN W. GOCKEL

CONCORDIA ®
PUBLISHING HOUSE
3558 SOUTH JEFFERSON AVENUE
SAINT LOUIS, MISSOURI 63118

Concordia Paperback Edition 1965

Concordia Publishing House, Saint Louis, Missouri

Copyright © 1961 by Concordia Publishing House

Library of Congress Catalog Card No. 61-13455

4 5 6 7 8 9 10 11 12 13   MAL   91 90 89 88 87 86 85 84 83 82

Manufactured in the United States of America

This volume is dedicated to

MILDRED

my beloved wife

A WORD TO THE READER

The past few years have seen many books published on the subject of anxiety. If the author of the present volume can claim any justification for the appearance of still another title in this rapidly expanding library, his justification will have to be found in the following three considerations. First, in the chapters of this book he has consistently limited himself to one highly specialized segment of the general field of anxiety. Secondly, he has approached this specialized field, not from the point of view of "religion in general," but from the point of view of one religion in particular. And finally, he has poured his material into a literary format which, it is his hope, will achieve a maximum of rapport between himself and the average reader.

The narrow segment of the field to which he has deliberately confined himself throughout the entire volume is that of spiritual anxiety. Still more specifically, he has limited himself to the inner stresses of *Christians!* In every chapter and on every page he is addressing himself to those members of the Christian church who, having made a sincere profession of the faith and having done their very best, with God's help, to live a life consistent with that profession, nevertheless find themselves the victims of those vague and frequently indefinable fears which are usually lumped together under the general head of spiritual anxiety.

His approach throughout is frankly that of classical, evangelical Christianity. For this he makes no apology. It was St. Augustine, that great sinner turned saint, who said: "Thou hast made us for Thyself, and our souls are restless until they find their rest in Thee." The rest which the human soul is seeking has a theological dimension, and it is the purpose of Christian revelation to address itself to that dimension. The spiritual unrest which grips the human heart is the result of a fractured vertical relationship, the relationship between the individual and his God; and it is Christianity's purpose to heal this fracture and thereby to bring health and gladness to the human soul.

Christianity brings health to the human soul through a message which is utterly unique, the product not of human research and inquiry, but of divine revelation. This message, completely unique to the Christian religion, gravitates, as it were, around two poles — that of sin and that of grace. Diagnostically, the Biblical message of *sin* strips the individual naked in the presence of his God and reveals him for exactly what he is — a rebel, an ingrate, a truant from the Father's house. Therapeutically, the Biblical message of *grace* directs the frightened truant to the Father's love as that love was demonstrated and authenticated by the incarnation, the atoning death, and the triumphant resurrection of His divine Son. It is particularly to the Biblical message of *grace* in its almost infinite variety of aspects that the author returns again and again throughout the pages of this book, as to an old and trusted apothecary whose shelves are stocked with healing medicines for the soul.

Let it be clearly stated, however, that the spiritual medicines offered in these chapters are not intended for all alike. As in the physical realm, so also in the spiritual, one man's medicine can well prove another man's poison. These chapters have been written specifically for the *spiritually anxious*. Had they been written for the spiritually callous, the spiritually indifferent, or the spiritually unconcerned, they would have been written entirely differently. The Bible makes a clear distinction in its approach to various types of people. To the spiritually callous or indifferent it speaks condemningly and threateningly of sin, holding out the sure prospect of ultimate and utter ruin. To the spiritually sensitive, to those who are spiritually concerned and anxious, it speaks comfortingly and reassuringly of God's mercy, love, and grace. It points them to Christ as the veritable embodiment of these loving and forgiving attributes of God. It holds out to them the sure hope of pardon for their sin and eternal fellowship with God through faith in His beloved Son. Both messages of Scripture have complete validity — the message of human sin and the message of divine grace — but since in these pages the author is addressing only the spiritually anxious, and not the spiritually callous, his emphasis is almost totally on *grace*. It is in the wonderful Gospel of God's grace, and not in the proclamation of His wrath, that all spiritual anxiety must find its ultimate answer.

The author has a wholesome respect for the psychiatric profession. Indeed, this very respect has prompted him not to indulge in any amateurish venture into a field which is not his own. He realizes that there are vast and difficult areas in the general field of anxiety into which the theologian is not qualified to probe and on which he should not presume to speak. Hence the very limited segment of this vast subject treated in these pages. Hence, too, the purely pastoral approach, as distinguished from the professionally psychiatric. That both approaches can frequently supplement each other is being amply demonstrated today. Especially is this true when both the vertical and the horizontal relationships of life are inextricably involved.

A few words on the literary format of this volume may prove of value. In order to achieve a certain intimacy and to establish a ready rapport between himself and the reader, the author chose to cast his material in a series of personal letters. All of these letters are addressed to "Mark." Who is Mark? That is a valid question. Mark, of course, is a number of people. He is, first of all, a composite of that faceless group of many thousands whose letters have crossed the author's desk during a radio and television ministry extending over the greater part of two decades, first with the international Lutheran Hour on radio and then with "This Is the Life" on television. Secondly, Mark is a composite of a few intimate friends who over the years have come to the author with their spiritual doubts and religious uncertainties. And finally, there is something of the author himself in Mark. Unless the author himself had experienced some of the anxieties which trouble Mark, he would have found it most difficult to identify himself empathically with the man to whom this volume is addressed.

Mark is a literary license. To which the author is quick to add that he has taken a liberty with this license! The liberty consists in this, that he has attributed to Mark more problems, more doubts, more anxieties than should normally be attributed to any one man. He decided to take this liberty for two reasons. First, to give the book the continuity and the coherence which it needed. Secondly, to do justice, cumulatively, to the theological content of the various letters. More than once, a letter in the second half of this volume had to lean heavily on the content of a letter in the first half in order to do justice to the subject at hand. This could not have been done had the various letters been addressed to various people. Hence the attribution of more spiritual difficulties to *one* man than should normally be done. For this the author begs the reader's indulgence.

To enable the reader to determine the specific focus of each letter before reading it, the author has preceded each letter with a brief quotation, presumably from Mark's previous correspondence. This quotation will appear at the top of the first page of each letter. It is hoped that this feature will make for more intelligent and more purposeful reading. The Scripture quotations are taken from the Revised Standard Version of the Bible unless otherwise indicated. The abbreviation "KJ" denotes the King James Version, while the abbreviation "P" denotes J. B. Phillips' *The New Testament in Modern English*. It is suggested that the anxious reader look up all indicated passages in his Bible and read them in their larger context. Ordinarily, *The New Testament in Modern English* is to be preferred.

It is the author's sincere hope and ardent prayer that the letters published in this volume will bring comfort, courage, and strength to the troubled heart of many an anxious believer.

THE AUTHOR

CONTENTS

Letters to an Anxious Friend

I · A Prayer for the Fitting Word

Dear Mark:

It has been a few days since I received your latest letter. Ever since reading it, I have been in much prayer, asking the Lord to guide me — giving me not only the proper insights but also the proper words — so that, as it were, I may speak directly from *His* heart to yours.

For after all, it is in His heart, and not in mine, that the answer to your various problems must ultimately be found. Fortunately, as Christians we do have access to the heart of God, at least to the extent to which He has revealed it to us in the pages of His Word. It is in that Word, the Bible, that I hope to find the answer to some of the thoughts that have been troubling you.

I was greatly humbled by the fact that you reposed sufficient confidence in me to open up your innermost fears and conflicts — as completely, as honestly, and as unashamedly as you did. I hope that I shall, at least in a measure, justify that confidence. Let me state frankly that I have no particular scholarly or technical skills which qualify me, above others, to go into the various problems you have raised. Indeed, I feel a definite incompetence in this respect. I am sure that there are others whose specialized training and technical skills qualify them much better to answer some of your questions.

I bring only two qualifications to the task. First, I do believe that I am sufficiently acquainted with my Bible to know what it has to say about some of the basic fears and conflicts that have been troubling you. And, secondly, I myself have had to live with many of the same fears and conflicts and have found no ultimate, no permanently satisfying, answer to them outside of the clear and simple assurances of Holy Writ. It is because I have lived very intimately with some of these fears that I think I can understand what you are going through at present.

Believe me, Mark, when I say that I am not a stranger to your present feelings. I myself have struggled with them through many a trying day and many an anxious night — but, always I have been able to fight them at least to a stalemate, if not to final victory, through faith in God's divine assurances. If I had not myself lived with some of the haunting fears which are troubling you — indeed, if I were not even *now* engaged in the daily battle with some of the very same anxious thoughts which are assaulting your soul — I do not believe that I could write an adequate reply to your letters. May God, therefore, guide me as, with His Spirit's help, I try to lead you into the arsenal of His Word to find the fitting weapon with which we *both* can fight the common battle.

I shall, of course, not be able to answer you in a single letter. Nor even in just a few. Your correspondence has raised too many points which call for rather extended replies. I have therefore decided to give you my answer in a series of letters — no doubt, some long and some short — in which I shall address myself to some of the matters you have mentioned. To give focus to my replies, I shall precede each one with a brief quotation from your correspondence, and I shall then do my best to give you a helpful reply.

Please, pray with me that "the God of all comfort" will in each case give me the fitting thought and fitting word, so that each letter may prove a spiritual blessing.

John

"I have no right to call myself a Christian. . . . If I really were one, I wouldn't be so filled with fear and doubt and worry."

II · You Are Not Alone

Dear Mark:

Your confession of "worry" came as no surprise to me. In saying that, I do not wish in any way to minimize the agony of heart and soul which, according to your letter, you have been enduring. I know only too well, both from personal experience and from my ministry to others, what a trial you are going through. Only those whose faith has been tested in the fiery crucible of inner doubt can know the torture of which you speak.

Nor, frankly, was I surprised that, because of your recurring feelings of insecurity and what you call a "haunting secret dread," you have begun to doubt your very Christianity. In our day of superficial religion, when peace of mind and positive thinking have in many instances been confused with personal salvation, it is not at all surprising that those who fail to achieve peace of mind or who find themselves the victims of negative thinking jump to the conclusion that they are not Christians. They reason very logically that if Christians are people who have "peace of mind," and if they themselves are constantly plagued by inner turmoils, then surely they cannot be Christians. But it is not, of course, as simple as that. Life is far too complicated to be reduced to any airtight syllogism. Furthermore, much will depend upon what we mean by the word "Christian," and much will depend upon what we mean by the words "peace of mind." I shall have much more to say about this in a later letter.

About all I hope to accomplish this evening is to assure you that you are not alone. There are many Christians, sincere believers, who are fighting the very same struggle which is now taxing your mental and physical and spiritual energies. They, too, are baffled by the seeming incompatibility of a personal Christian faith on the one hand and an ever-recurring fear or doubt or insecurity on the other. In some instances they, too, have given way to a conclusion born of despair — the conclusion that, since a child of God puts his faith in his heavenly Father, they must not be God's children, or else they would not be assailed by these fearful storms of uncertainty.

Some time ago a very religious woman wrote to my office, pleading for spiritual help in a moment of deep and dark spiritual depression. Perhaps if I quote a few paragraphs from her letter, you will see that her problem, while not exactly like yours, is still quite similar. "Please, help me," she writes. "I have tried to believe in God all my life, but if someone doesn't help me soon, I am going to lose my mind — that is, what's left of it. I've prayed and prayed, but it seems that God has never heard me. I have always considered myself a Christian, but I'm beginning to wonder. Of one thing I'm sure, nothing good has ever come from all my praying.

"My problem is hard to put into words, but I suppose, to be perfectly frank, it's simply a case of being afraid twenty-four hours a day — afraid to get up in the morning, because I know it will simply mean the same thing over: 'nerves,' a stomach full of butterflies, cold sweats, and the daily dread of meeting my boss, who is really a fine man but who gives me the jitters every time he walks into my office.

"I know this is silly. But I also know it's real, and it's terrible, and I won't be able to stand it much longer. What I want to know is, can I really believe in a loving God in heaven, can I really believe that I have been redeemed for time and for eternity through Jesus Christ, His Son, and still go on day after day, scared, nervous, jittery, getting no joy out of life, and sometimes wishing I were dead? Can I carry on like this and still consider myself a Christian?"

If this woman's problem were an isolated instance, I would not have dignified it with the prominence I have given it. The fact is, her letter, in its essential content, is typical of hundreds which have reached my desk during recent years.

A teen-age girl, evidently a sincere and devout believer, writes that she is troubled by the uneasy and discomfiting thoughts which continue to assault her — thoughts about the spiritual plight of her unbelieving parents and her unbelieving girl friends — and she wonders why *she* must be troubled by these debilitating thoughts, while the people she is worried about are so much happier and carefree than she is. A fear-ridden, guilt-stricken, remorse-filled young woman who has read almost all the books her pastor has given her and who says, "I believe in Christ as my Savior," is filled with panic at the thought that her conscience is never at ease and that perhaps God has turned His back on her forever. A middle-aged businessman who is an officer in his church and who says he knows the basic doctrines of the Christian faith "backwards and forwards" is almost paralyzed by secret fears which he hesitates to confide even to his pastor — fears concerning his own eternal destiny.

As I said, hundreds of letters like these have come to my desk. They have come from the rich and the poor, the learned and the unlearned, and from persons in various walks of life. Whatever the differences of these people may be in background, status, class, or color, it would seem that there are at least two characteristics which all of them have in common. They are "religious." And they are "anxious." They profess, no doubt with varying degrees of justification, to be believers in the Lord Jesus Christ; and at the same time they admit being the tortured victims of various kinds of anxiety. They are, or at least they sincerely *want* to be, devoutly religious; and yet they are worried — frankly, openly, terribly worried.

Are these people unusual? Are they exceptions? Are they special cases for whom the church must devise some special program of spiritual therapy? Generally speaking, I do not think so. There are, of course, exceptional cases which will call for exceptional approaches. (In some cases, the ministrations of the Christian Gospel will prove fruitless until the way has been prepared by a competent psychiatrist. Or, conversely, the therapy of the psychiatrist will remain without permanent results until it has been undergirded by the assurances of the Gospel. In such cases both approaches have a legitimate and important role to play.) But, speaking broadly, I would classify these people as not too far from "normal." If the truth were known, it is quite probable that millions of people today who are sincerely and devoutly religious, and who are putting forth every effort to practice their religion, are nevertheless troubled from time to time (or, at least, during various periods of their life) by perplexing doubts, by unnamed fears, and by deep anxieties. They are both Christian and they are — if I may use the word which occurs again and again in their letters — "nervous." I am using the word "nervous" very loosely, as it is commonly used by the average person to describe his inner feelings of uneasiness and insecurity.

Personally I see nothing self-contradictory at all in the concept of a nervous Christian. A man can be both anxious and religious. He can be both anxious and at the same time live in a state of grace, the recipient of God's abounding love and mercy. In fact, I would say that a person who says that he is never anxious, never worried, never "nervous" may not be nearly as religious as he thinks, for he is very probably lying when he says so.

I do not mean, of course, that Christianity has no answer for anxiety. It most certainly has. But I do mean that in an imperfect world of imperfect men it is idle to look for a godly man from whose heart the anxieties of this mortal life have been entirely banished. It is true that, theologically conceived, anxiety is a sin — at least, to the extent to which it involves a lack of trust in God. But where is the believer who never sins? Anxiety, like any other human imperfection, is a state of mind which calls for the grace of God for its forgiveness and for its only effective therapy — a grace which is always available to the believer in Jesus Christ. If it is true that Christians sin, and surely it *is* true,[1] then it should not surprise us to find Christians who on occasion are anxious, jittery, "nervous," and filled with fear; for these all-too-human emotions are the weights of the flesh from which not even the most devout believers have been entirely freed.

Perhaps one of the most humbling experiences for a middle-aged clergyman is to read some of the sermons he delivered early in his ministry. Some time ago I came across an old sermon which I delivered in my first parish on the well-known text: "Casting all your care upon Him, for He careth for you."[2] It was a carefully prepared oration, based on a thorough study of the Greek original. With great pedantry I pointed out to my unlettered congregation of sharecroppers that the Greek word for "care" was very similar to our modern word "anxiety," and with great authority I asserted that all of our anxieties will *disappear* the moment we lift them from our shoulders and place them on the shoulders of our loving Father in heaven. While I never said it in so many words, I left the definite impression with my hapless little flock that any person who, after hearing my sermon that morning, would insist on clinging to his fears and worries could hardly consider himself a Christian. Not only was I hopelessly naïve in presenting the matter as I did, but, looking back from the vantage of thirty years, I must say that I was downright cruel. Surely, I was wrong! And I ask forgiveness from every sensitive soul whom I wounded that morning.

It is a relatively simple matter for a seminary graduate with a freshly framed diploma on his study wall, with a lovely bride with whom he is still spending his honeymoon, with all the world still bright and filled with promise — it is a relatively simple matter, I say, for such a young man to speak of the folly, the futility, and the sinfulness of anxiety, and to leave the impression that the anxious person is not a Christian. But let him live another thirty years, let him visit the poor mother of three

[1] 1 John 1:8   [2] 1 Peter 5:7 KJ

hungry youngsters whose husband has just drunk up another pay check and who doesn't know how the rent will be paid or where her children's next meal will come from — I say, let him associate with the poor, the distressed, the downtrodden for the major portion of a lifetime, or let him minister to the anguished intellectual who is beset by doubt and fear and insecurity, and he will be happy to include the anxiety-ridden within the borders of the Kingdom. He will be happy to enfold them with the blanket of sweet charity and to speak to them of the divine assurance which lies *above* and *beyond* and *beneath* anxiety!

What I am trying to say in this letter, Mark, is that you *do* have a right to call yourself a Christian, despite the inner fears and worries of which you speak. I am not saying that your fears are right or good, or that you should not address yourself, with God's help, to the task of getting rid of them. God does not want you to be the helpless victim of your fears! He wants you to make progress in the direction of overcoming them. But He knows your heart. He knows that you are weak. He knows that fear and worry are bound in the human breast, and His attitude toward you is one of Fatherly compassion. It was a man who had traversed the deepest and darkest valleys of spiritual depression who wrote one of the most beautiful Psalms of our Bible. In the 103d Psalm David writes:

> The Lord is merciful and gracious,
> slow to anger and abounding in steadfast love.
> He will not always chide,
> nor will He keep His anger forever.
> He does not deal with us according to our sins,
> nor requite us according to our iniquities.
> For as the heavens are high above the earth,
> so great is His steadfast love toward those who fear Him.
> As far as the east is from the west,
> so far does He remove our transgressions from us.
> *As a father pities his children,*
> *so the Lord pities those who fear Him.*
> *For He knows our frame;*
> *He remembers that we are dust.*[3]

[3] Psalm 103:8-14

God knows you for the weak and frail human being that you are — just as He knows me with all of my infirmities. The glorious fact is that He is willing to accept us in our weakness. I imagine that if today we could look down from the throne of God into the hearts of the masses of humanity about us, including the hearts of those who are sincerely devout, we would see an almost endless sea, forever restless with the churning waves of countless fears. But, looking from the throne of God, we would also be looking with the eyes of infinite compassion. For, make no mistake about it, God loves us — even with our worries.

No, you are not alone, Mark. There are many of us with you. The fraternity of the fearful is larger than you think. Thank God that, through Christ, the fraternity of the fearful is included in the fraternity of the redeemed. And as the redeemed of Christ, we can do something about our deepest fears.

Of this I shall write more later.

John

"If the Christian religion is true, why do I have this constant inner struggle, this almost endless conflict inside of me? Some of my friends, who are not Christians, seem to have more inner peace than I."

III · More Than Peace of Mind

Dear Mark:

The second statement which I have quoted from one of your letters may sound somewhat similar to the first. But in reality it is quite different. The first read: "I have no right to call myself a Christian. . . . If I really believed, I couldn't be so filled with fear and doubt and worry." The second reads: "If the Christian religion is true, why do I have this constant inner struggle, this almost endless conflict inside of me? Some of my friends, who are not Christians, seem to have more inner peace than I."

In the first instance, it was your personal faith that you were calling into question. In the second instance, it is the Christian religion itself. Now I shall not undertake within the brief scope of a single letter to present a defense of the Christian faith. In fact, strictly speaking, I couldn't do so if I *wished* to. The Christian faith is not something which we humans are called upon to defend. It is rather something which God's Holy Spirit plants and nourishes in individual human hearts. And He does so through the simple witness of His Word. Nothing that I could say or write could add a jot or tittle to the effectiveness of that witness. But I do feel that I can be of help to you by clearing up a misconception or two which may be standing in your way.

First, put away from your mind, now and forever, the thought that the ultimate purpose of human life on this earth is to achieve "peace of mind" — and that Christianity is a quick and easy road to that desired end. It is a cruel perversion of the Christian faith to palm it off as a tranquilizer sent from God, to regard it as a sort of happiness pill, or to peddle it (or to buy it) as a sort of spiritual anesthetic which will put all our inner struggles to rest. Peace of mind is *not* man's ultimate purpose on earth, nor is it the ultimate purpose of the Christian faith.

I hope that I will not shock you by what I am going to say. But if I do, please withhold your final judgment until later in our correspondence, when I shall have had ample opportunity to place this statement into a broader context. I have associated with quite a few people in my life, both Christian and non-Christian, and when it comes to what has popularly been called "peace of mind," I have sometimes seen much more of it in the life of the worldling than in the life of the Christian. I have seen rank unbelievers live from day to day, seemingly without a worry in the world, and I have seen dedicated Christians wrestling with inner spiritual problems of which the worldling could not possibly have had the slightest awareness. I have known the spiritually unconcerned to go to bed at night and "sleep the sleep of the dead" until morning and then get up hale and hearty and full of vigor, while the spiritually sensitive man has tossed all night and has brought a tired and weary body to the tasks of the new day. Of one thing I am sure: peace of mind, in the sense in which this term is popularly used today, is more within the grasp of the worldling, the unbeliever, or the spiritually unconcerned than it is within the grasp of the Christian who takes his religion seriously.

Perhaps right here I should also make another statement which will run counter to some popular conceptions of the Christian faith. Not that I want to be shocking just for the sake of being shocking, but I think it is important that we clear away some generally held misunderstandings from the very outset.

It is not the purpose of Christianity to produce "adjusted personalities," completely freed from inner tensions. Nor is it the purpose of Christianity to help the individual "adjust" to the world in which he lives by removing the day-to-day frictions which are bound to result from his contacts with the world. If by an "adjusted personality" we mean a person who has come to peace with himself and with the world about him in such a way that both inner and outer conflict has ceased, then I am afraid that the Christian is of all personalities the most maladjusted. This lies in the very nature of the world and in the very nature of the Christian. According to the Bible they are, and always will remain incompatibles. For the Christian, life in this world is not so much a matter of adjusting as it is a matter of resisting. And in the very attitude and act of resisting there must needs be conflict. As the Bible puts it, "Do not be conformed to the world but be *transformed*." [1] And for the transformed individual in an untransformed world there will inevitably be conflict. In fact, for many who were the first to espouse the Christian faith, it meant opposition, persecution, and finally violent death. They were the most "maladjusted" people of their day.

I know that you have been a faithful student of your Bible and that you have therefore developed an intimate acquaintance with the apostle Paul. No one, I am sure, will deny that he was among the greatest Christians that ever lived, and that he was used by God as perhaps no other human for the founding and spreading of the Christian church. Here was a man who literally gave his all for the cause of the Gospel, finally offering up his life on the altar of devotion to the Christ who had died for him. Truly, a man among men, a man miraculously used by God to accomplish God's purposes. Yet no one who has become intimately acquainted with this spiritual giant would dare to say that he was a man of inner poise, that he had been freed from the piercing pain of inner struggle, or that he had developed "a way" with people which had circumvented friction or unpleasantness. On the basis of what we know of him from the Book of Acts and from his various epistles, I think we are justi-

[1] Romans 12:2

fied in picturing the apostle Paul as a nervously brittle man, not too well "adjusted" by this world's standards, somewhat emotional, and the periodic victim of deep and dark anxiety.

True, Paul was a brave man when the defense of his Gospel called for spiritual courage, confessing his faith even in the presence of kings.[2] Nevertheless he did not have the serene self-composure or self-confidence which one might have expected of a man with his unquestioned intellectual ability and undoubted spiritual conviction. In later years he wrote to the believers in Corinth: "I was with you in weakness and in much fear and trembling."[3] He was keenly aware of his own inadequacy for the task before him, and as a result he approached it with an inner trepidation which, from his own admission, we may well assume made itself visible by a physical trembling. In other words, Paul knew what it meant to have the jitters — and to let his jitters show. No doubt, many a twentieth-century practitioner would have told the apostle: "Come on, Paul! Snap out of it! You've got an inferiority complex. What you need is to feed your ego. There's no point in admitting to weakness or fear or trembling. Those are negative thoughts. Get rid of them! Above all, as a religious man you should be able to surmount such feelings of inadequacy. What has become of your much-publicized boast 'I can do all things through Christ which strengtheneth me'?"[4]

To be sure, Paul would have had an answer for such cheerless cheerleaders, and I hope that, cumulatively, I shall be able to unfold his answer bit by bit in our correspondence. For the time being, however, let me pin down this important (and to some, disconcerting) fact: one of the greatest exponents of the Christian faith since the ascension of Christ into heaven was a man of inner fears and uncertainties which, despite his best efforts, he never fully overcame.

Some of Paul's most agonizing moments came to him just *because* of insights which were his as a Christian. They were conflicts of soul which he would never have known, had he not become a follower of Christ. To mention only one, Paul carried a continuing burden in his heart because of his fellow Jews whose

[2] Acts 26   [3] 1 Corinthians 2:3   [4] Philippians 4:13 KJ

eyes were blinded to the truth of the Gospel. Listen to his own description of this burden: "I have great sorrow and unceasing anguish in my heart," he says, "for I could wish that I myself were accursed and cut off from Christ for the sake of my brethren, my kinsmen by race." [5] Because of the spiritual plight of his countrymen, of which *he* was aware but of which *they* weren't, his heart was filled with "great sorrow and unceasing anguish," or as Phillips translates these words of Paul, "it is like a pain that never leaves me." Had Paul never become a Christian, he would never have known this pain. He would never have become the victim of this inner anguish, for his heart would have remained insensitive to the spiritual needs of his brethren.

Perhaps it may seem that I am straying somewhat far afield. Let me remind you of the statement in your letter which occasioned my line of thought this evening. You said: "If the Christian religion is true, why do I have this constant inner struggle — this almost endless conflict in my soul? Some of my friends, who are not Christians, seem to have more inner peace than I." All that I am trying to establish at this point, before going into the specific nature of *your* inner conflicts, is that you need not be surprised that inner conflicts do persist, even in the heart of the most devout. The conscientious believer in the Christian Gospel knows of conflicts of which the insensitive worldling has never even dreamed.

The apostle Paul makes his most dramatic and, to you and me, his most comforting confession of inner conflict in his well-known seventh chapter of Romans. I shall have more to say about this chapter in a future letter, but let me anticipate a little here. In this chapter he admits, or perhaps I should rather say he *asserts*, that ever since he became a Christian there has been a constant war going on inside of him. This is the war between his sinful nature, that is, the nature he received at birth, and the new nature which was given him by God's Holy Spirit at the time of his conversion. These two natures, he says, are waging a constant war within him. Nor is it only a cold war which Paul describes, a war with both adversaries sitting sullenly and glowering at each other. No, it is a hot war, a bloody war, a knock-

5 Romans 9:2

down-and-drag-out affair. For Paul this inner civil war is so painfully distressing that, after describing it to his fellow Christians at Rome, he exclaims: "Wretched man that I am! Who will deliver me from this rickety old body which houses these warring factions?" Remember, it is the apostle Paul, one of the greatest of all Christians, who is making this abject admission!

Let me quote only a few of the concluding verses of this remarkable chapter of Paul's Letter to the Romans. He writes: "So I find it to be a law that when I want to do right, evil lies close at hand. For I delight in the law of God in my inmost self, but I see in my members another law at war with the law of my mind and making me captive to the law of sin which dwells in my members. Wretched man that I am! Who will deliver me from this body of death?" [6] I would suggest that you read the entire chapter to see how Paul describes the perpetual struggle which inevitably must go on in the Christian heart, the struggle between the two "laws," the Law of God and the law of sin, or the two natures, the one which is ours by birth and the one which is ours by rebirth. From this struggle there is no exemption this side of the grave.

(Lest I leave you with the wrong impression at this point, let me hasten to assure you that in the midst of these inevitable conflicts there is an ever-present *peace* for the Christian. But this peace has nothing at all in common with the "peace" of which you read so much today. It is a peace which in its very nature is beyond the grasp of the nonspiritual man, a peace whose supernatural ingredients lie completely outside the knowledge of the unconverted mind. It is a peace in the midst of war, a calm in the midst of turmoil, a tranquil citadel at the very center of life against which the storms of doubt and fear and anxious thoughts can only dash and break their fury, but into which they can never enter. You will recall the Savior's promise to His disciples: "Peace I leave with you; My peace I give to you; *not as the world gives* do I give to you." [7] The peace which the Christian finds in Christ is something "wholly other" than the superficial peace concerning which we humans usually speak. It is the heaven-sent, confident assurance of which the apostle

---

[6] Romans 7:21-24   [7] John 14:27

Paul spoke when he wrote to the Philippians: "And the peace of God, *which passes all understanding,* will keep your hearts and your minds in Christ Jesus." [8] I am really getting ahead of my story in this parenthesis. I do not want to expand this point any further here. But I did not want the trend of these first few letters to imply that there was nothing left for the Christian but a fatalistic submission to the inevitable tensions of life. No, he has something far more positive than that. I shall have a great deal more to say on this score later.)

In the fourth chapter of Paul's Second Letter to the Corinthians he has a remarkable description of himself and of his colaborers in the Christian Gospel. It is not a very rosy picture. Surely, not a picture of men for whom life had rolled out the red carpet. Let me quote just a few verses. He says: "We are afflicted in every way, but not crushed; perplexed, but not driven to despair; persecuted, but not forsaken; struck down, but not destroyed; always carrying in the body the death of Jesus, so that the life of Jesus may also be manifested in our bodies." [9] The people to whom Paul wrote these words lived in a city of luxury and pleasure, a city notorious for its licentiousness and self-indulgence. Corinth was a gay metropolis, the Hollywood of ancient Greece. But in the midst of Corinth's gaiety and carefreeness Paul and his friends were "afflicted . . . perplexed . . . persecuted . . . struck down . . . always carrying in the body the death of Jesus." Don't think for a moment that Paul was complaining when he wrote these words. He was merely listing his credentials (and those of his colleagues) as consistent and conscientious believers in Christ's Gospel. And these are *still* the credentials of the man who has taken his stand with Christ: "afflicted, but not crushed . . . perplexed, but not driven to despair . . . persecuted, but not forsaken . . . struck down, but not destroyed."

Later in this same letter Paul comes back to this identical thought. Again speaking of himself and of those who were standing by him in the proclamation of the Christian Gospel, he says: "We are treated as impostors, and yet we are true; as unknown, and yet well known; as dying, and behold we live; as punished,

---

and yet not killed; as sorrowful, yet always rejoicing; as poor, yet making many rich; as having nothing, and yet possessing everything." [10] Are these various phrases contradictions in themselves? Yes, in a sense. In another sense, no. When put together, they depict the inevitable tensions of the Christian life. Negatively, there are the attributes: "impostors . . . unknown . . . dying . . . punished . . . sorrowful . . . poor . . . having nothing." Positively, there are the attributes: "true . . . well known . . . behold we live . . . not killed . . . always rejoicing . . . making many rich . . . possessing everything." If these two lists of attributes sound contradictory — and certainly, in a sense, they do — they serve only to underscore the inescapable "contradictions" in the thought and life of the Christian. He is both sorrowful — in that his life is one of daily contrition and repentance for sin; and he is always rejoicing — in that he knows that his God is a God of love and that, through Christ, his sins have been forgiven. He is both poor — in that he is painfully aware of his nothingness before God; and yet he makes many rich — in that he is used by God to bring the comfort of the Gospel to others. He has nothing — in that he has surrendered his all at the foot of the cross; and yet he possesses everything — in that, through Christ, he possesses vast spiritual blessing in this life and limitless spiritual treasures in the life to come.

Surely, a life concerning which so many "opposites" are true will not be a life that is free from inner tensions. It will rather be a life which is characterized by a constant tug, a constant pull, yes, a constant *conflict*, between these two aspects of the Christian life. If you tell me that a Christian is a sorrowful person, I will have to agree with you — in a certain respect. If you tell me that a Christian is a joyful person, I will also have to agree with you — in a certain respect. And I shall be speaking of the same Christian. For it is true that he is "sorrowful, yet always rejoicing." This is the inevitable contradiction of the Christian life. In a very real sense, every Christian is in himself a contradiction; and because he is, he is living in a constant tension between these two aspects of his nature. As I shall point out later, this is the inevitable conflict of a religion of Law and Gospel, of sin and grace.

[10] 2 Corinthians 6:8-10

Remember, the only point which I am trying to make tonight is simply this: the Christian religion is not a guarantee of peace of mind in the sense in which most people speak today, nor is it a way of life which always makes for ease and pleasantness. More often than you may think, its results are just the opposite.[11] The fact that you are experiencing inner struggles in your religious life does not mean that Christianity has let you down, nor does it mean that Christ's Gospel is not true. On the contrary, some of the spiritual struggles which you mention in your letter are an indication to me that the Holy Spirit is at work in your heart and that you are being led to a deeper and clearer knowledge of Jesus Christ as Lord and Savior. The spiritually dead have no spiritual problems. It is the spiritually alive who must fight the incessant battles of the spirit against the flesh.

I feel confident, Mark, that when the present storm subsides, you will see that God was in it. In fact, I pray that even in the midst of the storm you will be given a clearer vision of Him who even now is your faithful Pilot and who will surely stand by you until the clouds are lifted. Won't you commit your anxious heart to Him right now and pray:

> As a mother stills her child,
> Thou canst hush the ocean wild;
> Boist'rous waves obey Thy will
> When Thou say'st to them, "Be still!"
> Wondrous Sovereign of the sea,
> Jesus, Savior, pilot me!

John

11 Matthew 10:34

"Sometimes it seems to me that tragedy is at the very heart of the universe. Could this be true?"

IV · This World We Live in

Dear Mark:

You have asked a question which has been debated by philosophers since time immemorial. "Is tragedy at the heart of the universe?" The very fact that men have been asking this question down through the centuries is in itself significant. Evidently they were aware of enough tragedy both in their own lives and in the world about them to consider this question relevant and to consider its discussion purposeful. I realize that for you, too, this is not an academic question. You have asked it because in your own life you have been brought face to face with sufficient tragedy to wonder whether or not tragedy is of the essence of human existence.

Strangely enough (or *was* it really strange?), the apostle Paul grappled with this question too. In his letter to the Christians at Rome he speaks of the sufferings of this present life in their relation to the glories of the life to come; and in doing so he touches on the very matter you have broached: *is* tragedy a part of the essence of life? Let me quote a substantial section from that letter. Since both the King James and the Revised Standard Version of this passage are somewhat difficult, I shall quote from J. B. Phillips' well-known paraphrase:

"In my opinion," says Paul, "whatever we may have to go through now is less than nothing compared with the magnificent future God has planned for us. The whole creation is on tiptoe to see the wonderful sight of the sons of God coming into their own. . . . The hope is that in the end the whole of created life will be rescued from the *tyranny of change and decay,* and have its share in that magnificent liberty which can only belong to the children of God.

"It is plain to anyone with eyes to see that at the present time *all created life groans in a sort of universal travail.* And it is plain, too, that we who have a foretaste of the Spirit are in a *state of painful tension,* while we wait for that redemption of our bodies which will mean that at last we have realized our full sonship in Him. We are saved by this hope, but in our moments of impatience let us remember that hope always means waiting for something that we haven't yet got. But if we hope for something we cannot see, then we must settle down to wait for it in patience. The Spirit of God not only maintains this hope within us, but helps us in our present limitations." [1]

I have italicized three statements in the above quotation, and please remember that this quotation is taken from a page of your Bible. The first statement is that, in our present life, we are living under a "tyranny of change and decay." The second is that "at the present time all created life groans in a sort of universal travail," the picture being that of a mother in physical distress as she gives birth to a child. And the third is that we Christians who have already been given a foretaste of the glories which will be ours when Christ returns to claim us as His own are "in a state of painful tension." Or as the Revised Standard Version has it, we "groan inwardly."

Evidently the apostle Paul, as the other Bible writers, would have answered your question, "Is tragedy of the essence of human life?" with an emphatic and unquestioning affirmative. Yes, tragedy *is* at the heart of life on this planet! In fact, the whole earth with everything on it and in it, both animate and inanimate, is "subject to the bondage of corruption," to use

[1] Romans 8:18-26 P

a phrase from the King James Version. And as long as you and I are living in this world, we shall forever be caught up in the tragedy which lies at the heart of human life.

This tragedy, of course, which is at the very center of human existence, is, as you and I know it, the tragedy of *sin*. Now, don't think of sin as being merely a theological abstraction, something concerning which theologians like to spin fanciful theories which are entirely unrelated to life. Sin and life are inseparable. Go where you will, and you will find the wreckage, the ruin, and the rubble of human life which lie in the wake of sin like blasted homes and broken bodies in the path of a tornado: our crowded hospitals, in which bed space is at a premium and in which each bed could tell a hundred stories of sorrow, anguish, and despair; our penal institutions, filled to overflowing; our divorce courts, with their hour-by-hour reports of unhappiness and misery, broken homes, unwanted children; the daily headlines of crime, brutality, adultery, and sordidness. Or just look into the daily lives of ordinary people and see what anguish the tragedy of sin has wrought: quarreling, bickering, cantankerousness; fear, worry, insecurity; envy, jealousy, discontent; selfishness, pride, arrogance; friction, contention, enmity; unemployment, disability, poverty; sickness, pain, and death. And remember that, according to the Bible, all these tragedies had their root in the *ultimate* tragedy of human history, the tragedy of sin. It is because of sin, that universal catastrophe which has every human being in its grip, that all life on this planet is, in the words of Paul, under "the tyranny of change and decay," and that "all created life groans in a sort of universal travail," and that we Christians must remain in "a state of painful tension" until Christ, our Savior, returns to rescue all of His redeemed.

I know that there are those who deny that tragedy is at the heart of human life. I am not prepared, nor, perhaps, am I equipped, to discuss this question with them philosophically. But I *am* prepared to point to the Biblical drama of redemption as proof sufficient for the believing Christian. No one who contemplates the crucifixion of Jesus Christ with a reverent and believing heart can ever doubt that tragedy is inextricably interwoven into the very warp and woof of the human story. Why should Innocence have been nailed to a cross? Why should Omnipotence have bowed in ignominious defeat? Why should Truth have succumbed to falsehood? Why should the Prince of Life have been laid into a tomb? Why should God have died?

You and I know the answer, Mark. Because of sin, God sent His only Son into a world of rebels, a world which had declared its independence from Him, a world which was in a state of defiant insurrection against its own Creator, even as it is today. For, make no mistake about it, man as he is by nature is *still* in revolt against God, and therein lies the tragedy which is at the very heart of human life. Man's revolt against his Maker, and the divine curse upon man's revolt! You and I have contributed our share to that revolt and, although by God's wonderful grace in Christ we have been completely forgiven, we are still living in a world which is estranged from Him. We are still living in a world which has tragedy at its heart and, until Christ comes to rescue us from it, we shall have to face up to this stern reality.

Is this really anything so surprising? Didn't Christ Himself say: "In the world you have tribulation"? [2] (I shall leave for a later context the fact that He followed these words immediately with the strengthening assurance: "But be of good cheer, I have overcome the world.") Didn't He say: "If any man would come after Me, let him . . . take up his *cross* and follow Me"? [3] And didn't Paul, that great man of tragedy on the one hand and heroic faith on the other, remind the early Christians that "through many tribulations we must enter the kingdom of God"? [4] This last statement, by the way, takes on additional significance when we remember that it was spoken a few days after Paul's enemies had stoned him and dragged his body out of the city and left him lying on the ground, supposing that he was dead. "Tribulations" indeed!

Yes, Mark, tragedy *is* at the heart of this world of sin. And, as you no doubt have learned, life has a grim way of reminding us of this painful truth from day to day. It would be idle for us to try to laugh this stubborn fact out of court. It would be

[2] John 16:33   [3] Matthew 16:24   [4] Acts 14:22

ostrich-folly for us to fall in with the "peace of mind" exponents and try to whistle this inexorable fact of life into oblivion. The tragedy is there. We stub our toes and bump our knees against it every day. Sometimes we are painfully hurt. Sometimes we are crushed. So powerful, so omnipresent, so all-pervading is the tragedy which lies at the heart of a world which is under sin!

I need not tell you that I had a constructive purpose in writing this particular letter as I did. From your question I gathered that you perhaps thought that tragedy was *not* a universal ingredient of human life. To doubt this fact is one of the surest roads to despair. He who feels that tragedy is unique with him is likely to be of all men most disconsolate. Nothing is so crushing as a sense of aloneness in misfortune. But I had also another constructive purpose. Until we recognize the root *cause* of human tragedy, we shall never be able to cope with it. I wanted to be sure that you saw the essential human tragedy in its worldwide context — in man's rebellion against his Maker. In sin! It is at that level that Christianity has something to say to your problem. Christianity *does* have the answer to sin, man's basic tragedy. And by that token it also has the answer to all the smaller tragedies of life. Of this I shall write in a later letter.

John

V · The God Whom Christ Revealed

Dear Mark:

You ask: "Can there really be a God of love?" Of course, I understand the reason for your question. When you wrote it, your mind was filled with what seemed to be convincing evidence to the contrary. And, indeed, it is not difficult to find such "evidence" — without even looking for it. Why would a God of love make a madhouse like this crazy, mixed-up world in which we live? Why would a God of love permit a world of poverty and hunger, hatred and strife, war and pestilence, fear and anxiety, to go on tumbling to its doom?

I shall have to admit that, if I were to take counsel only with my reason, my answer could only be the echo of my question: *why?* There is much, very much, in the world today which unenlightened human reason simply *cannot* reconcile with man's conception of a God of love. But right there, Mark, is the rub. Each of us is tempted to pit the world in which we live against our *own* conception of a god of love — the kind of god our reason would create. As Christians, we have disavowed such a god. Ours is a God so far above human reason that we do not try to measure Him or box Him in by the limitations of our finite intellect.

Ours is the God, not of reason, but of revelation: the God who, as it were, has revealed just enough of Himself to us to let us know that His ultimate intentions for us are good. "My thoughts are not your thoughts, neither are your ways My ways, says the Lord. For as the heavens are higher than the earth, so are My ways higher than your ways and My thoughts than your thoughts." [1] In other words, God in His inner essence, and also in many of His dealings with the human race, is utterly unsearchable for you and me. I am sure you also remember those striking words with which the apostle Paul concluded one of the profoundest chapters of his Letter to the Romans: "Oh, the depth of the riches and wisdom and knowledge of God! How unsearchable are His judgments and how inscrutable His ways! For who has known the mind of the Lord, or who has been His counselor?" [2] God did not call any of us in for advice, either on how to create the world or on how to run it. Nor has He seen fit to reveal more of His purpose and plan to us than His divine wisdom dictates.

But the amazing fact remains that He *has* revealed Himself to us — in the pages of inspired Scripture and pre-eminently in the person and work of Jesus Christ, His Son. In this unique revelation He has revealed Himself to us as a *God of love*. True, He has also revealed Himself as a God of holiness, righteousness, and justice. In a different context I would feel called upon to emphasize these attributes of the Deity and to show how humanity has brought its own miseries on itself by rebelling against these very attributes of God. I touched upon this in my previous letter. Right now I am confining myself specifically to your question: Can there really be a God of love?

I suppose that whether or not a person believes that God is a God of love, would depend upon what he thinks the world *needs* the most from God — and whether or not God has filled that need. The man who thinks that the supreme need of human life is physical health, and that there can be no gift that is greater, will find it difficult to believe in a God of love when he walks through a crowded ward at the city hospital. The man who believes that the greatest need of the human race today is

[1] Isaiah 55:8, 9   [2] Romans 11:33, 34

international peace, and that there is no gift that is greater, will find it difficult to believe in a God of love as he sees nations poised on the brink of mutual destruction. The sweet young thing who has come to regard her beauty as the ultimate gift of God to her will find it difficult to believe in a God of love if her face is miserably scarred in an auto accident. Or the prosperous businessman who has come to regard his soaring stocks and bulging bank account as the ultimate of divine blessings will find it difficult to believe in a God of love if by a sudden stroke of misfortune he is reduced to poverty. It all depends upon what we consider the world's — and our own — greatest need, and whether or not we believe that God in His goodness has filled that need.

According to the Christian revelation there can be no doubt as to what is man's greatest need. Nor can there be any doubt as to whether or not God has filled that need. The greatest need of every human being, alienated and estranged as he is from his Maker, is *reunion* with God. Until that reunion has been effected, he is adrift, at loose ends with himself, and at odds with his Maker. He is "lost," cut off from the only Source of availing help. Still worse, he is under the righteous judgment of the holy God against whose will he has rebelled. "By nature children of wrath, like the rest of mankind" [3] is the way the Bible puts it. Until a person has been reconciled and reinstated into the family of God, all the pleasures of life are like ashes in his mouth. Until he knows for sure that he has been accepted back into the Father's bosom, and that no power on earth or in hell will ever be able to separate him from the Father's arms again — I say, until *then* he is missing out on mankind's greatest and most pressing need: reunion, reconciliation. Or if I may use that simple word which lies at the very heart and center of the Christian Gospel: his greatest need is *forgiveness.*

Or do you doubt that reunion with God, reconciliation with the divine Creator and Judge, is the basic need of man? Make no mistake about it, Mark, the basic need of man is theological or, to use the simpler word, religious. Man is a creature made *by* God and *for* God, and until he has come into a proper

---

[3] Ephesians 2:3

relation *with* God, his basic need in life remains unfilled. He is cut loose, adrift. Consciously or unconsciously, he is a runaway, far from home. Not only does he not know the way back, but he is desperately afraid to return. Whether he admits it or not, he is afraid to return to the God on whom he has turned his back. And so he stumbles aimlessly, uncertainly, *anxiously* from one day into another — not sure of the object of his fear, sure only that at the center of his life there is a dread which makes genuine peace of soul impossible. St. Augustine once put it this way: "Thou hast made us for Thyself, and our souls can find no rest until they find their rest in Thee."

It is in relation to this basic need of men that God has chosen to reveal His love in fullest measure. What you or I could never have done by ourselves, God chose to do for us. He chose to bridge the gap between Himself and us. He sent His only Son into the world to pay the price of our rebellion, to bring about a complete and perfect reconciliation, to earn for us the full and free remission of our sins. Out of the fullness of His love He decided to go all the way, to give up the very best He had, in the Person of His divine Son. And this divine Son, out of infinite compassion for a race which was at odds with its Maker, went all the way to pay the price of reconciliation. He died in the place of you and me, assumed our penalty, and restored a truant race to the loving bosom of His Father. That, as you know, is the central message of our Bible.

I need hardly remind you of such Scriptural assurances as the words of Christ: "God so *loved* the world that He gave His only-begotten Son, that whosoever believeth in Him should not perish, but have everlasting life." [4] Or the well-known words in the First Epistle of St. John: "To us, the greatest demonstration of God's love for us has been His sending His only Son into the world to give us life through Him. We see real love, not in the [alleged] fact that we loved God, but that He loved us and sent His Son to make personal atonement for our sins." [5] It was because the God of heaven had gone all the way to redeem a fallen race through Jesus Christ, that Paul could end several of his epistles to the early Christians by commending them to "the God of love." [6]

[4] John 3:16 KJ   [5] 1 John 4:9 P   [6] 2 Corinthians 14:11

Now, does all of this perhaps sound somewhat academic in the face of your present problem? Does a "God of love" who sent His Son to earth almost two thousand years ago to expiate your sins seem more like a theological concept than a present Friend? Does this whole business of spiritual redemption seem irrelevant to your present dark mood, your anxiousness about today, tomorrow, and life in general? I know that for some people it is very difficult to establish a connection between the Biblical message of "God's love in Christ" and the day-to-day problems of this workaday world. Yet the Bible establishes a very definite connection between the two. After describing the security of the man who has been safely anchored in God through Christ, Paul asks: "In face of all this, what is there left to say? If God is for us, who can be against us? He that did not spare His own Son but gave Him up for us all — can we not trust such a God to give us, with Him, everything else that we can need?" And then he goes on:

"Who would dare to accuse us, whom God has chosen? The Judge Himself has declared us free from sin. Who is in a position to condemn? Only Christ, and Christ died for us, Christ rose for us, Christ reigns in power for us, Christ prays for us!

"Can anything separate us from the love of Christ? Can trouble, pain, or persecution? Can lack of clothes and food, danger to life and limb, the threat of force of arms? Indeed some of us know the truth of that ancient text:

'For Thy sake we are killed all the day long;
We were accounted as sheep for the slaughter.'

"No, in all these things we win an overwhelming victory through Him who has proved His love for us.

"I have become absolutely convinced that neither death nor life, neither messenger of Heaven nor monarch of earth, neither what happens today nor what may happen tomorrow, neither a power from on high nor a power from below, nor anything else in God's whole world has any power to separate us from the love of God in Jesus Christ, our Lord." [7]

Notice the tremendous confidence which runs through this

[7] Romans 8:31-39 P

entire passage. Paul is ready for anything that might happen today or tomorrow, no matter how good or how bad. And why? Because he has been assured of a love that will never change. It is the love of God, revealed by the sending of His Son for the redemption of the world. Paul's logic in this passage is simply this: If God has given us the Gift, surely He will also let us have the ribbons. If He has given us His Son to die for us, to ransom us from the spiritual powers that held us in bondage and to win us back to eternal fellowship with Him, then surely He will find a way for us to surmount all of life's minor tragedies. If He has done the greater thing, surely He will also do the smaller. "He that did not spare His own Son but gave Him up for us all — can we not trust such a God to give us, with Him, everything else that we can need?"

It is this God, the Father of Jesus Christ, our Lord, who says to you and to me: "I have loved you with an everlasting love; therefore I have continued My faithfulness to you." [8] Yes, Mark, our God *is* a God of love, no matter how many "evidences" to the contrary we may see about us. He has shown us just enough of His good and gracious will toward us to let us know that He harbors "thoughts of peace and not of evil" toward us His children. It is true, He has left much of His plan and purpose for your life and mine undisclosed. There is a long wall without any windows along which you and I must walk, but there *is* a window at the far end of the corridor — and through that window we see the rays of His redeeming love. Let us not so much complain about the blank wall where we now are standing; let us rather thank Him for the light of the Gospel which shines down the darkened hallway from the far end, assuring us that He is there and that His attitude toward us is one of Fatherly affection.

Sometimes I am asked: "What difference is there between an anxious or a frightened Christian on the one hand and an anxious or a frightened unbeliever on the other? Aren't they both anxious? Aren't they both afraid?" The question is a valid one, and I believe that there is a valid answer. A sick and feverish child may cry out in the night for the comfort of its mother. Usually it will cease its sobbing as soon as it feels her

[8] Jeremiah 31:3

arms around him. It is enough to know that Mother is close and that her love is there to comfort and sustain. The sickness and the fever may persist, but the feel of mother-arms around the feverish body is sufficient for the moment. Could Mother be there — and serious harm still befall? Must not the present harm ultimately yield to good, as long as Mother stays? The sick child is still sick, but, oh, what a difference to know that beneath and around it are the arms of Mother's love!

So, too, the Christian. As long as he lives in this world, he will know what it means to be sick — sick in body, mind, and spirit. And for reasons known only to God, some of these periods of stress will last longer than he seems able to endure. But in the midst of his trial he will know the comfort of the sick child in the arms of his mother. He will know that, frail and fragile as he is, he is still safe in the arms of a loving God. Still sick? Still anxious? Still filled with a myriad of little fears? Yes, perhaps, because he is still a weak and sinful human. And yet, beneath his fears, like the quiet deep of the ocean beneath the churning surface waves, is the calm assurance that the God of love is with him and that even this trial, in God's inscrutable providence, will ultimately be for his good.

Yes, Mark, there *is* a God of love — the God who has revealed Himself to us through Jesus Christ, His Son. It is the God whom you have known since childhood. He is your God today even as He was then, and He will continue to be your God throughout the years to come. Today He speaks to you, as He does to every believing heart, and says:

> Fear not, for I have redeemed you;
> I have called you by name, you are Mine.
> When you pass through the waters, I will be with you;
> and through the rivers, they shall not overwhelm you;
> When you walk through fire, you shall not be burned,
> and the flame shall not consume you.
> For I am the Lord, your God.[9]

There will be floods to pass through and fires to walk through, but He who has redeemed you and called you by your name will be with you — for *you are His.*

John

9 Isaiah 43:1-3

"I say I believe in God, in Christ, and in salvation through faith in Him, but sometimes I wonder if I really do. If I do, my faith is surely weak."

VI · When the Wick Burns Low

Dear Mark:

There is a beautiful passage in the Book of Isaiah which reads: "A bruised reed He will not break, and a dimly burning wick He will not quench."[1] This, as Matthew points out in his Gospel, was both a prediction and a description of the Savior whom God was to send into the world.[2] More important for you and me right now is the fact that this is a description of *your* Savior, the mighty Champion to whom you have entrusted yourself, body and soul, for time and for eternity. "A bruised reed He will not break." What does that mean? It means that a slender reed that has been bruised or a tender twig that has been scraped or badly bent will never be broken in His hands. Rather, He will straighten it and bind it and nurse it and summon His omnipotence to sustain and extend its life. "And a dimly burning wick He will not quench." What does *that* mean? It means that a wick in an oil lamp which is sputtering and smoking and on the verge of going out, He will not extinguish. Rather, He will trim it, adjust it, supply new oil, and call upon His omnipotence to keep the flame alive.

[1] Isaiah 42:3   [2] Matthew 12:20

Your faith, Mark, may at times seem to be that battered reed, bruised to the point of breaking; or it may seem to be that smoking wick, ready to sputter its last. At moments like that, just remember the kind of Savior you have. "A bruised reed He will not break, and a dimly burning wick He will not quench." He is not going to let your faith run out. He will nurse it, nourish it, and sustain it. Never forget that it was He who gave you your faith in the first place,[3] and our Lord is no Indian giver.[4]

The problem of a weak faith, I know, has been a source of concern and distress to many whose faith temporarily is clouded by doubt. Like the man in the Gospel, their secret prayer to God is: "I believe! Help my unbelief!"[5] The man who prayed that prayer received the thing he prayed for — not only the healing of his son but also, we can be sure, the healing of his unbelief. Above all, Mark, let's never lose sight of the fact that as far as our soul's salvation is concerned, as far as our adoption into the family of God and our ultimate entry into eternal life are concerned, a weak faith saves us just as surely as a strong one. A ten-dollar gold piece is a ten-dollar gold piece, whether in the frail hand of an infant or in the strong hand of a giant. The weakness or the strength of the hand that holds it does not in any way affect its worth, nor does it in any way alter the fact of ownership. In the one case, the weak hand owns it; in the other, the strong. Both own the thing they hold. Similarly, a weak faith possesses all of the riches of God's love and mercy *right now;* and in God's own good time it will enter into the full fruition of every Gospel promise, when faith (even weak faith) will have been turned to sight.

Sometimes, I'm afraid, we confuse the faith that *saves* with the faith that *dares,* as though we were saved by some kind of heroic act, the courageous achievement of a dauntless spirit. Faith thus becomes synonymous with courage. It is true, the word faith does sometimes have that meaning. But if *that* were the faith of which the Bible speaks when it says that we are saved by faith, I am sure that none of us could ever be sure of our salvation. I am sure that every Christian has known days when his "faith" (in the sense of a courageous, dauntless spirit)

[3] Ephesians 2:8   [4] Hebrews 12:2   [5] Mark 9:24

has been anything but heroic, when his valor and his spiritual fervor have been at a very low ebb. Indeed, if we take faith as a synonym of spiritual valor, how often has every one of us lost faith!

No, the faith that ushers us into the presence of God, that makes us His own for time and eternity, is anything *but* heroic — in the sense in which we usually think of that term. It is the front side of the coin the opposite side of which reads "despair." The faith that saves is the faith which despairs of self utterly and completely and which clings to the one Person in all the world who can help. And that Person is Jesus Christ. And what is it about Christ to which it clings? It clings to His Saviorhood, of course. To His substitutionary death and resurrection in our place, in our behalf! To the redemption which He won for us on Calvary's cross! To the reconciliation He accomplished between His Father and us! It looks to the opened gates of heaven, opened wide by His blood-stained hands! It looks to His outstretched arms and trusts His inviting voice: "Come unto Me, all ye that labor and are heavy laden, and I will give you rest." [6] It rests in His indescribably sweet assurance: "My sheep hear My voice, and I know them, and they follow Me; and I give them eternal life, and they shall never perish, and no one shall snatch them out of My hand. My Father, who has given them to Me, is greater than all, and no one is able to snatch them out of the Father's hand. I and the Father are one." [7]

Saving faith is a resting in that promise, as a child rests its weight in its mother's arms. In days of storm and stress it is a *clinging* to that promise — and to the Promisor — as a drowning man clinging to the outstretched hand of the strong man come to save him. In reality, as I shall point out later, it isn't our faith that saves us at all. It is God who saves us. Faith is merely the puny hand with which we reach forth and make His marvelous salvation ours. Puny though the hand may be, the salvation which it appropriates is great beyond description.

The apostle Paul describes the great salvation which can be "laid hold of" even by a puny faith in his well-known words to the Christians at Rome: "Therefore, since we are justified by

[6] Matthew 11:28 KJ   [7] John 10:27-30

faith, we have peace with God through our Lord Jesus Christ. Through Him we have obtained access to this grace wherein we stand, and we rejoice in our hope of sharing the glory of God. More than that, we rejoice in our sufferings, knowing that suffering produces endurance, and endurance produces character, and character produces hope, and hope does not disappoint us, because God's love has been poured into our hearts through the Holy Spirit which has been given to us." [8] Did you notice what was the doorway to this cathedral of love and joy and strength? Faith! And what kind of faith? The faith that justifies. And what kind of faith is that? The simple, childlike trust in the Saviorhood of Jesus Christ. That was the whole drift of Paul's letter to the Romans. Faith, be it large or small, strong or weak, is the door of access to "peace with God through our Lord Jesus Christ" and to "this grace wherein we stand."

I cannot look into your heart, Mark, yet I have every assurance that you are standing in that grace. Your sensitivity to God's will for you, your years of fellowship with Christ and with His church, the eloquently unspoken prayer which breathes silently through all your letters "I believe. Help my unbelief" — all of these are evidences of the working of the Spirit. Your faith may, indeed, be "a dimly burning wick," but it is a wick and it is burning, and the breath of God's Holy Spirit will not only keep it alive but, in His own good time, will again blow it into full flame.

I am reserving for a later chapter several of the things God expects of you — exercises, as it were — to keep the flame of faith alive, to nourish and to feed it. My purpose tonight is merely to assure you that even a weak faith is a saving faith and that, even now, troubled by inner doubts as you are, you have peace with God through your Lord Jesus Christ, and that you are standing in His wonderful grace. You are *His* — forgiven, restored, and reinstated, because of Calvary.

John

[8] Romans 5:1-5

"I am constantly haunted by the fear that someday I shall lose my faith and that I shall be eternally lost."

VII · Your Hand in His

Dear Mark:

The fear which you mention has troubled many a devout believer. It is the fear of outliving our faith, of living to see the day when we no longer have the confidence that, through Christ, God is our loving Father and that salvation is ours through childlike trust in Him. Many a believer has been deeply concerned lest the faith which is his today be gone tomorrow, lest the faith of his youth take wings and desert him in his old age, lest, when he is called upon to walk through the valley of the shadow, he find that he has no faith to which to hold.

The haunting question is: how can I be sure that I shall have the willingness or the strength or the spiritual capacity to *believe* at those great moments in my life when the issues of time and eternity are finally decided? How can I be sure that I will not "let go" just at the moment when I should "hold on," and thus forfeit the salvation which I have found in Christ and which I am enjoying today?

The question is, indeed, a serious one and, for a person of your sensitivity, not at all unusual. I shall do my very best to answer it, not on the basis of any unique or extraordinary insights of my own, but solely on the objective assurances of God's Word. But let me begin by telling you a little story which will lead very naturally to the Bible's answer to your problem.

On a cold winter day, when the sidewalks were covered with ice, a pastor and his little boy were on their way to church. It was the first time three-year-old Bobby was wearing an overcoat in which there were deep pockets. As they approached a slippery place, the father extended his hand to the youngster and said: "You'd better let me hold your hand." But the boy's hands were snug in his pockets, and he kept them there — until he slipped and fell! Somewhat humbled by this experience, he raised himself and said: "I'll hold your hand, Daddy." And he reached up and took his father's hand with the feeble grasp of a three-year-old.

Soon they came to another slippery place — and down he went! His tiny fingers had not been able to grip his father's hand with sufficient strength to insure against his fall. Once more he picked himself up and they resumed their walk. But after a moment's reflection Bobby looked up into his father's face and said with childlike confidence: "*YOU* hold *MY* hand, Daddy." And as they went safely on their way and ultimately reached their destination, it was the *father's* hand that upheld the lad and preserved him from further danger. *Not the boy's grip on the father's hand, but the father's grip on his!*

Similarly, Mark, your continuing in the faith is not so much a matter of your holding on to God as it is a matter of God holding on to you. And you have His promise that He will. Let's begin by asking just where you got your faith in the first place? Was it by some superheroic act of your own? Was it by lying awake at night or by working at it long hours during the day? Not at all. Your faith in God as your loving Father and in Christ as your loving Savior and in eternal life through His death for you — that faith was, and continues to be, a free and unmerited gift of God. Do you remember that passage in Ephesians? I shall quote it in its entire context so that the jewel which is imbedded at its center will stand out in all of its intended glory. Paul writes: "But God, who is rich in mercy, out of the great love with which He loved us, even when we were dead through our trespasses, made us alive together with Christ . . . and raised us up with Him, and made us sit with Him in the heavenly places in Christ Jesus, that in the coming ages He might show the immeasurable riches of His grace in kindness toward us in Christ Jesus. For by grace you have been saved *through faith; and this is not your own doing, it is the gift of God* — not because of works, lest any man should boast. For we are His workmanship, created in Christ Jesus for good works, which God prepared beforehand, that we should walk in them." [1]

Did you notice how in the opening verses of the above passage God is always the Subject and we the object? It is He that does all the doing. It is He that has made us alive in Christ. It is He that has raised us up and enabled us to take our place with Christ in the enjoyment of heavenly blessings. It is He that wants to show us the immeasurable riches of His grace. And when finally "we" become the subject in this remarkable passage, the verbs suddenly change to the passive. We have been saved by His grace, through faith — through a faith that is not of our own doing but which *He has given us.* Our faith is not our accomplishment, but His. We are, in whole and in all our parts, His workmanship, created "for good works, which God prepared beforehand, that we should walk in them."

If there is one thing that the Bible, especially Paul in his epistles, makes very clear, it is the fact that our faith is not a product of our own effort. It is not even the result of our own choosing. It is from start to finish a gift of God's 'unmerited grace. I always liked that passage in the King James Version of the Bible which called Jesus "the Author and Finisher of our faith." [2] He is the One who created it, and He is also the One who sustains it and brings it to perfection. Writing to his Philippian Christians, Paul says: "He who began a good work in you will bring it to completion at the Day of Jesus Christ." [3] He is referring here to the faith which had been created in the hearts of the Philippians by the operation of the Holy Spirit. He says that God began it and that God will complete it. St. Peter gives expression to the same immovable conviction. He says: "By His great mercy we have been born anew to a living hope, through the resurrection

[1] Ephesians 2:4-10   [2] Hebrews 12:2 KJ   [3] Philippians 1:6

of Jesus Christ from the dead, and to an inheritance which is imperishable, undefiled, and unfading, kept in heaven for you, who *by God's power* are guarded through faith for a salvation ready to be revealed *in the last time*." [4] To Peter, the final and complete salvation of the believer was as sure as God's own Word is sure. It is an inheritance, "imperishable, undefiled, and unfading," reserved in heaven for us. And God is guarding not only the inheritance but also the inheritors, His children, in whose favor He has written His testament. They are guarded "by God's power," which has engendered faith in their hearts and which will preserve that faith until "the last time."

You see then, Mark, it is our gracious God, not you or I, who will preserve us in the faith until the day of His appearing. (Shortly, I shall point out that God has appointed specific means whereby He works on human hearts and whereby He creates and sustains this faith. Right now, however, my purpose is to draw your attention away from that puny hand of yours whereby you are trying to hold on to your salvation, and to focus your attention on the omnipotent hand of God which is holding you and behind which there is the eternal promise of the Almighty, the promise of His grace and mercy revealed in Jesus Christ, your Savior.) To me the most beautiful and the most eloquent assurance of our continuing in the faith is to be found on the lips of the Savior Himself. As usual, He avoided the involved and technical terminology of the theologian and used a simple illustration, familiar to the people of His day. I am referring to those wonderful words of His: "My sheep hear My voice, and I know them, and they follow Me, and I give them eternal life, and they shall never perish, and no one shall snatch them out of My hand. My Father, who has given them to Me, is greater than all, and no one is able to snatch them out of the Father's hand." [5] Could there be anything more beautiful, more reassuring? Remember, it wasn't John or Paul or Peter who spoke those words. It was Christ. And He was speaking of His sheep, His followers, those who have put their trust in Him, those who have committed their souls to His care and keeping. Of them He says, "they shall never perish, and no one shall snatch them out of My hand." It isn't the sheep, Mark, who guarantee their own safety by cling-

[4] 1 Peter 1:3-5   [5] John 10:27-29

ing to the shepherd's hand; it is the shepherd whose strong grasp holds on to the sheep and prevents them from being snatched by thieves or wolves. I know that ever since you were a child you have committed your life, your eternal destiny, to Jesus Christ as Lord and Savior. Could He, the Good Shepherd, ever relax His hold on you?

There is another approach to this problem which is troubling you, this fear that you may outlive your faith in Christ as Savior. If there is one attribute which the New Testament ascribes to God above all others, it is the attribute of love. It is true, the Bible also speaks of God as being just and holy and righteous, and if I were writing to someone else, someone who is smug and spiritually self-satisfied, I might find it necessary to stress these very attributes of God. But the tone of all your letters to me indicates very clearly that, far from being smug, you are deeply troubled about your spiritual condition. For you, and for all like you, the Christian Gospel emphasizes the love of God as His dominant attribute. Just read the Gospel of John and his epistles. These were addressed to believers, to the "society of the concerned," to those who had been crushed by the thought of God's holiness and justice and of their own unworthiness and who had thrown themselves completely on His grace and mercy, as revealed in Jesus Christ. To them he speaks incessantly of God's love. It is John who wrote simply and profoundly: "God is Love." [6] The God who sent His only-begotten Son into the world to rescue you and me for all eternity is, above all else, the God of love. The entire plan of salvation by which God redeemed the human race was conceived in love, carried out in love, and on the day of Christ's return in glory will be consummated in love. God loved the world (you and me) so much that He gave us His only Son. Christ, the Only-Begotten of the Father, loved the world (you and me) so much that He laid down His life upon the cross for us so that we might be eternally free. The Holy Spirit loved the world (you and me) so much that He brought us to faith in Christ as Savior and planted into our hearts the witness of salvation. The Holy Trinity — Father, Son, and Holy Spirit — loved the world (you and me) so much that

[6] 1 John 4:16

this our gracious God presented us with a full, free, complete, and perfect salvation.

And now the question. Could a God of love offer us a salvation which was anything less than perfect? Could He offer us a salvation which was not complete, a salvation that wouldn't "wear"? Could a God of love mock us with a counterfeit salvation which would fail us when we needed it the most? No, if He is a God of love (and both Christ and the Bible assure us that He is), then the salvation which He has given us in the Christian Gospel is a salvation which goes all the way. Not only our coming to faith, not only our continuing in faith, but also our dying in the faith — all are part of the Gospel promise and the Gospel call which you and I have heeded. Ours is not a bargain salvation, not a cheat, not something which will serve a while and then leave us in the lurch. Our salvation, the Bible assures us, is complete, final, perfect. And being complete, it includes not only the gift of faith which was ours yesterday, not only the gift of faith which is ours today, but also the gift of faith which will be ours tomorrow and until our journey's end. The God of the Gospel would be less than the God of love if He had not included our *perseverance* in the faith in the gift of salvation which He freely offers.

St. Paul knew this. In his great eighth chapter of his Letter to the Romans he was speaking of the believer's perseverance in the faith as a part of the gift which the God of love bestows. Although I have quoted at length from this chapter in one of my previous letters, I shall spell out a substantial section of it once more, because I believe that right now you need the very assurance which it can give you. I shall quote it in the translation by J. B. Phillips. Please remember, Mark, that what I am about to quote is the Bible, not an interpretation of the Bible, not a book about the Bible, but *the* Bible, God's own Word to you and me, especially His Word to you in answer to your present questions. He says:

"Moreover, we know that to those who love God, who are called according to His plan, everything that happens fits into a pattern for good. God, in His foreknowledge, chose them to bear the family likeness of His Son, that He might be the eldest of a family of many brothers. He chose them long ago; when the time came, He called them; He made them righteous in His sight and then lifted them to the splendor of life as His own sons.

"In face of all this, what is there left to say? If God is for us, who can be against us? He that did not spare His own Son but gave Him up for us all — can we not trust such a God to give us, with Him, everything else that we can need?

"Who would dare to accuse us, whom God has chosen? The Judge Himself has declared us free from sin. Who is in a position to condemn? Only Christ, and Christ died for us, Christ rose for us, Christ reigns in power for us, Christ prays for us!

"Can anything separate us from the love of Christ? Can trouble, pain, or persecution? Can lack of clothes and food, danger to life and limb, the threat of force of arms? Indeed some of us know the truth of that ancient text:

'For Thy sake we are killed all the day long;
We were accounted as sheep for the slaughter.'

"No, in all these things we win an overwhelming victory through Him who has proved His love for us.

"I have become absolutely convinced that neither death nor life, neither messenger of Heaven nor monarch of earth, neither what happens today nor what may happen tomorrow, neither a power from on high nor a power from below, nor anything else in God's whole world has any power to separate us from the love of God in Jesus Christ, our Lord!" [7]

It is true, in this marvelous passage Paul says nothing explicitly about continuing or persevering in the faith, but implicit in every word is the fact that God is not going to let you and me down, He is not going to let us fall from grace, He is not going to let us outlive our faith and thus forfeit our eternal inheritance. He has chosen us. He has called us. He has implanted saving faith into our hearts. He has declared us righteous in His sight because of the merits of His Son. And He is not going to let anything happen that would separate us from the divine love which has made all of this possible. He has in truth gone all the way.

[7] Romans 8:28-39 P

I'm sure you remember Martin Luther's familiar explanation of the Third Article of the Apostles' Creed. He says: "I believe that I cannot by my own reason or strength believe in Jesus Christ, my Lord, or come to Him; but the Holy Ghost has called me by the Gospel, enlightened me with His gifts, sanctified and *kept* me in the true faith; even as He calls, gathers, enlightens, and sanctifies the whole Christian church on earth and *keeps* it with Jesus Christ in the one true faith; in which Christian church He daily and richly forgives all sins to me and all believers, and will at the Last Day raise up me and all the dead, and give unto me and all believers in Christ eternal life. This is most certainly true."

I have italicized the two words "kept" and "keeps," since behind them lies the divine assurance you are seeking. Who is it that keeps you in the faith? Not you! Not all your agonizing, not all your spiritual wrestling, not all your moral striving. No, it is the Holy Spirit of God who has brought you to the faith and who is keeping you, according to God's own promise. As Paul says, "He who began a good work in you will bring it to completion at the Day of Jesus Christ." [8]

This letter would be incomplete and misleading if I were to end it here. It would be wrong to picture our salvation as the act of a capricious God who has reached down from heaven and, willy-nilly, by an act of His omnipotent hand put certain people into a salvation deepfreeze, reserved for eternal glory at the Day of Judgment. Our salvation is the result neither of divine caprice nor of divine omnipotence. It is the result of a divine plan which issued from divine love. I shall have more to say about the divine plan (of redemption and ultimate salvation) later, but the one aspect of God's plan which I believe I should mention in this letter is what you have learned to know as "the means of grace." It is vital to the problem with which you are presently concerned, the fear of someday losing your faith in Christ and being eternally lost.

God did not give you your faith through an act of magic, nor will He keep you in it by an unsheathed act of His omnipotence. Both in the giving and in the keeping He has chosen to

[8] Philippians 1:6

act through *means* — means of His own choosing. Those means are His Word: the preached Word of His Gospel and the visible Word of His sacraments, Baptism and the Lord's Supper. It was through His Word that He brought you to faith, and it will be through His Word that He keeps you in faith. Do you remember that striking statement of St. Peter? Writing to the early Christians who were scattered throughout Asia Minor, he reminded them: "You have been born anew, not of perishable seed but of imperishable, through the living and abiding Word of God. . . . That Word is the good news [the Gospel] which was preached to you." [9] True, the birth of faith in their hearts had been accomplished by God, but God had accomplished it through His chosen means — "the living and abiding Word," "the Gospel," the good news of the life and death and resurrection of Jesus Christ on man's behalf. You will recall, in Luther's explanation of the Third Article of the Apostles' Creed, which I quoted on a previous page, he said: "I believe that I cannot by my own reason or strength believe in Jesus Christ, my Lord, or come to Him; but the Holy Ghost has called me *by the Gospel.* . . ." The Gospel of Christ is the powerful means by which God has created faith in your heart. It was the same Gospel, the good news about Christ, that had transformed faithless Saul into faith-filled Paul. That is why he could write to the Romans: "I am not ashamed of the Gospel of Christ, for it is the *power of God* unto salvation." [10] St. James attributes the same power to the Gospel of Christ when he urges us to "receive with meekness the implanted Word, which is *able to save your souls.*" [11]

Similarly, it is God, working through His Word, who will keep us in the faith. The aged St. John, toward the close of his life, wrote to the believers of his day: "Let what you heard from the beginning [the Gospel] abide in you. If what you heard from the beginning abides in you, then you will abide in the Son and in the Father. And this is what He has promised us, eternal life," [12] As long as we are still on this side of eternity, abiding in the Father will mean abiding in His Word, in His promises of grace and pardon and life everlasting through His beloved Son. This is a clear New Testament doctrine. Of the

[9] 1 Peter 1:23-25   [10] Romans 1:16 KJ
[11] James 1:21   [12] 1 John 2:24, 25

early Christians we read that "they devoted themselves to the apostles' teaching and fellowship, to the breaking of bread and the prayers." [13] The Word of God was central in their lives. And together with their preoccupation with the Word went a fellowship with others whose lives were centered in the same revelation of God's love.

But why have I extended this letter to include these thoughts on the importance and the power of the Word? Because I did not want to leave you with the impression, Mark, that your continuing in the faith is something automatic — as though a person could say (as I know you wouldn't!): "Well, now that God has brought me to faith, I can really 'live it up.' I can do just as I please. I have His assurance that, no matter what I do, my faith will never die." No, that would be a misuse of the Biblical assurance. God, in His unsearchable wisdom, has tied our faith to His Word. He has tied our faith to His Gospel. He has tied our faith to His Christ.

My closing counsel to you, therefore, is that you stay close to His Word, close to His Gospel, close to His Christ; that you cultivate the habit of daily meditation on His precious promises; that you continue your splendid record of regular church attendance; that you participate thoughtfully and meaningfully in the prayers of the Christian congregation; that you listen attentively to your pastor's sermons, which are expositions of the Word; that you neglect no opportunity to partake of the Lord's Supper for the strengthening of your faith and the reassurance of the peace and pardon which is yours in Jesus Christ, your Savior; that you seek every opportunity for fellowship with those whose lives are centered on the Word, and that morning, noon, and night you speak to Him who has already spoken to you and has given you His pledge: "I will never fail you nor forsake you." [14]

In His Word He is reaching out His strong arm and His strong hand to you. Don't be afraid to put your puny faith into His hand. And remember, it will not be your puny faith that does the holding — it will be the strong grip of His hand.

John

---

[13] Acts 2:42   [14] Hebrews 13:5

VIII · Your Guilt on Him

Dear Mark:

From time to time you have referred to your "feelings of guilt" and to the anguish of mind you have suffered because of these recurring feelings. I wish it were possible for us to get together and to talk this matter out. There is so much that I should know before I presume to speak. If these feelings which torment you are attached to certain wrongs that you have done and of which you are clearly and regretfully aware, I am sure that I can help you. In fact, that is what a Christian pastor is for — to speak the word of *pardon*[1] in the name of Christ.[2] The Christian religion does have the answer to objective, palpable guilt. It does have the answer to the stricken conscience which is assailed by the bitter memory of conscious wrong.

Unfortunately, the human mind has a way of playing cruel tricks. It can trap us in a web of *imaginary* guilt, from which escape is a slow and painful process, perhaps calling for the technical skill of a competent psychiatrist. Imaginary guilt or subjective guilt can be much more difficult to deal with than *real* guilt, since its roots are usually bedded in the hidden recesses of the subconscious. I doubt, however, that yours is a case of

[1] Matthew 18:18   [2] 2 Corinthians 5:18-21

imaginary guilt. I would rather assume, from our lengthy correspondence, that yours is a case of a sensitive conscience, the kind of conscience which made the apostle Paul cry out in anguish: "Wretched man that I am! Who will deliver me from this body of death?" [3] and which made him confess that he was the "foremost of sinners." [4] It lies in the very nature of things that the spiritually minded person will be more aware of his sins than will the unspiritual.

In the early days of our country an evangelist was preaching at an outdoor meeting. A flippant young man interrupted him and mockingly said: "You talk about the burden of sin. I've never felt it. How heavy is it?" The startled preacher paused momentarily and then replied: "Tell me, if you laid a hundred-pound weight on a corpse, would it feel the load?" The youth sneered: "No, of course not, because it's dead." To which the preacher answered: "And that spirit, too, is dead which feels no load of sin." A keen awareness of sin, far from being an indication of our *far-ness* from God, can very well be an indication of our *closeness* to Him.

The Bible calls King David a man after God's own heart.[5] And surely anyone who reads the Psalms of David will agree that he was a man who lived in close and intimate communion with his Maker. Yet there were periods in this great man's life when his guilt loomed up before him like a frightening monster, when his conscience roared its relentless accusation, when, as he put it, "my body wasted away through my groaning all day long." [6] I'm sure you remember the psalm which he wrote after he had committed a particularly grievous sin, a psalm which has proved a model prayer of penitence for guilt-stricken sinners ever since:

> Have mercy on me, O God,
> according to Thy steadfast love;
> according to Thy abundant mercy
> blot out my transgressions.
> Wash me thoroughly from my iniquity
> and cleanse me from my sin!

[3] Romans 7:24   [4] 1 Timothy 1:15   [5] 1 Samuel 13:14
[6] Psalm 32:3

> For I know my transgressions,
> and my sin is ever before me.
> Against Thee, Thee only, have I sinned
> and done that which is evil
> in Thy sight! [7]

David had a particular sin in mind when he prayed that prayer — a sin which, if it had remained unforgiven, would have made life utterly unbearable for him.

If there is a particular sin which is bothering you right now, Mark, may I encourage you to do just what David did in his great prayer of confession — open your soul to God, stand naked in His presence, confess the sin which is robbing you of peace, and ask for His forgiveness. He has promised to forgive you. As the God of love and never-ending faithfulness, He will never break a promise. David found that out. Many of his psalms are hymns of unrestrained *joy*, hymns of gratitude and praise — gratitude especially for the undeserved forgiveness which he had experienced so abundantly. Listen to this same man shout for joy:

> Bless the Lord, O my soul;
> and all that is within me,
> bless His holy name!
> Bless the Lord, O my soul,
> and forget not all His benefits,
> *who forgives all your iniquity,*
> who redeems your life from the pit,
> who heals all your diseases,
> who crowns you with steadfast love
> and mercy,
> who satisfies you with good as
> long as you live,
> so that your strength is renewed
> like the eagle's. [8]

Remember, the man who sobbed, "Have mercy on me, O God" is the same man who sang, "Bless the Lord, O my soul; and all that is within me, bless His holy name!" How could one man

[7] Psalm 51:1-4   [8] Psalm 103:1-5

utter *both* of these prayers? Because he had learned to know
and to trust the God "who forgives all your iniquity" and "who
crowns you with steadfast love and mercy." This is the same
God whom you have learned to know by faith and who has
entered into a sacred agreement with you, sealed in the blood
of His only-begotten Son [9] — the agreement of full and free forgiveness for each and every sin. He has never gone back on that
agreement, Mark, and He never will.

I realize that in our most penitent moments it is difficult to
believe that a holy God would consent to overlook our repeated
transgressions. How can our sinfulness stand in the presence of
His righteousness? How can our uncleanness stand in the presence of His purity? How can our crookedness, our falseness,
our hypocrisy, our duplicity stand in the presence of His all-
seeing and all-knowing justice? How can *we* stand in the presence of — *Him?* I'm sure you know the answer, Mark. None of
us could stand in the presence of the holy God, if it were not
for Jesus Christ, His Son. Our sins had thrown up a wall of
separation between our God and us. But God broke down that
wall through the life and death and resurrection of His only-
begotten Son.[10] As the Bible puts it: "God was in Christ, reconciling the world to Himself, not counting their trespasses
against them." [11]

How was this reconciliation accomplished? I need hardly
remind you. The Bible tells us: "Surely He hath borne our griefs
and carried our sorrows. . . . He was wounded for our transgressions, He was bruised for our iniquities; the chastisement of
[or which brought about] our peace was upon Him; and with
His stripes we are healed. . . . The Lord hath laid on *Him* the
iniquity of *us* all." [12] St. Paul put the entire Christian Gospel into
five short monosyllables when he wrote: "Christ died for our
sins." [13] St. Peter preached the same Gospel when he wrote:
"Christ Himself bore our sins in His own body on the tree
[cross]." [14] St. John expressed the same conviction when he
wrote: "If anyone does sin, we have an Advocate with the
Father, Jesus Christ the Righteous; and He is the expiation [the

---

[9] Matthew 26:28   [10] Ephesians 2:11-21   [11] 2 Corinthians 5:19
[12] Isaiah 53:4-6 KJ   [13] 1 Corinthians 15:3   [14] 1 Peter 2:24

full payment] for our sins, and not for ours only but also for the sins of the whole world." [15] And the Savior Himself, while instituting the Lord's Supper on the night before His crucifixion, said: "This is My blood of the covenant, which is poured out for many for the forgiveness of sins." [16] These passages, and many more, tell us how our reconciliation with God was brought about, how our forgiveness was achieved — namely, through the substitutionary death of His beloved Son in our place.*

Or do these passages sound like theological abstractions to you, something which has little or no relation to life as it is being lived, especially to *your* life? Believe me, Mark, these passages of Scripture have a very real relation to you in your everyday living. They are the very air which God expects you and me to breathe if we are to wage a successful war against the germs of guilt which have a way of growing in our heart. They are the soul-cleansing, life-giving thoughts with which we are to suffuse our thinking every morning, noon, and night. "Christ died for our sins!" "Christ died for our sins!" "Christ died for our sins!" Go to sleep with that thought every night. Awake with it every morning. Take it with you to your work. And remember, God has told you that since His Son *has* died for your transgressions, your soul is free!

God does not expect you to wage a losing war with your conscience. He does not want you to be cowed by its insistent clamoring. He has put into your hands and into your heart a weapon which can effectively silence the cunning and cutting voice of the accuser. Perhaps the simplest way of showing how a believer in Christ can stop the mouth of his mocking conscience is to listen to an imaginary conversation between a believer and the merciless accuser which lurks in every human breast. This, or something similar, is what we would likely hear:

Conscience: You have sinned!

Believer: Where have I sinned?

Conscience: You have broken all of God's commandments. You haven't loved Him with all your heart and soul and mind. You haven't loved your neighbor as yourself. You've dealt un-

[15] 1 John 1:1, 2   [16] Matthew 26:28   * See Chapter xix

fairly with your parents, unfairly with your children. You've hated, you've cheated, you've slandered, you've been jealous. You've harbored unclean thoughts, spoken unclean words, become guilty of unclean deeds. You've been selfish, greedy, graspy. You've been more concerned with making a good living than making a good life. Again and again you've played the part of the hypocrite — even your good deeds were frequently only a sham. You've ignored God. You've left Him out of much of your thinking. You've. . . .

Believer: I agree with every word you say. I'm guilty. I'd be a fool and a liar if I'd try to deny it.

Conscience: And you know what God says about people who do such things. "Cursed be everyone who does not abide by all things written in the Book of the Law, and do them." [17] And "the wages of sin is death." [18]

Believer: Yes, I know. I know that I have sinned, and I know that a righteous God (if He is to remain righteous and if He is to remain God) must punish every transgression of His righteous will.

Conscience: Therefore you are lost!

Believer: Ah, that's where you are *wrong!* God in His mercy has provided me with a Substitute. This Substitute has assumed my guilt. He has paid my penalty. When He died on the cross, He suffered the pangs of eternal hell for me. And when His Father raised Him from the grave on the third day, He tore up my summons and promised that I shall never be haled into the court of heaven for any misdeed I have done. Because Christ, my Substitute, has made good for me, I have been declared innocent, *guiltless,* in the sight of His Father. Begone, conscience! I have work to do.

The dialog, of course, is imaginary. But the argument which lies beneath it is the eternal truth of your heavenly Father, Mark. Listen to these words of Scripture. "There is therefore now no condemnation for those who are in Christ Jesus." [19] "For He

---

[17] Galatians 3:10   [18] Romans 6:23   [19] Romans 8:1

hath made Him to be sin for us who knew no sin." [20] "And the Lord hath laid on *Him* the iniquity of *us* all." [21] "Who would dare to accuse us now, whom God has chosen? The Judge Himself has declared us free from sin." [22] These are the assurances of God Himself to you and me. God wants us to lift our heads high, to throw our shoulders back, and to walk erect — as free men, breathing the fresh, clean air of His grace, reveling in the pardon which is ours through Him who loved us. [23]

Perhaps I should add a word here about the possibility of an *oversensitive* conscience — or should I say, a conscience which is sensitive about things concerning which it need not be. Again and again I have met people who are living with an uneasy conscience while, if they would only open their eyes to the truth, they would see that there is no reason at all for their uneasiness. They have magnified little things which have no intrinsic moral implications into matters of life-and-death importance. There are many things in life, Mark, which are in themselves completely neutral as far as their moral rightness or wrongness is concerned; and we shall only make ourselves of all men most miserable if we insist on investing each of these with moral significance.

The great God of heaven is not concerned about whether I lace my shoes in the morning with a single or a double bow. All else being equal, He is not concerned about whether I drink coffee or postum for breakfast; whether I eat meat or abstain from meat; whether I chew gum or smoke a pipe; whether I drink a glass of wine before retiring or drink a cup of hot milk; whether I play a game of bridge with my friends or express a preference for chess; whether I join in a square dance or go on a hayride; whether I relax and go to a good movie or stay home and read a book. None of these things have any moral implications in themselves and we shall succeed only in storing up unnecessary "guilt feelings" if we insist on making moral issues out of them.

One of St. Paul's purposes for writing his letter to the Christians at Colossae was to warn them against certain "blue noses"

[20] 2 Corinthians 5:21 KJ   [21] Isaiah 53:6 KJ
[22] Romans 8:33 P   [23] Romans 5:1-5

in their midst who were trying to subvert the Christian Gospel by a long list of dos and don'ts. Listen to how Paul approaches this problem. He writes: "You who were spiritually dead because of your sins . . . God has now made to share in the very life of Christ! He has forgiven you all your sins: Christ has utterly wiped out the damning evidence of broken laws and commandments which always hung over our heads, and has completely annulled it by nailing it over His own head on the cross. . . . In view of these tremendous facts, *don't let anyone worry you by criticizing what you eat or drink,* or what holy days you ought to observe, or bothering you over new moons or Sabbaths. All these things have at most only a symbolical value: the solid fact is Christ. . . . Why do you take the slightest notice of these purely human prohibitions — *'Don't touch this,' 'Don't taste that,'* and *'Don't handle the other'*? 'This,' 'that,' and 'the other' will all pass away after use! I know that these regulations look wise with their self-inspired efforts at worship. . . . But in actual practice they do honor, not to God, but to man's own pride." [24]

To Paul, Christianity was not a series of dos and don'ts (don't eat this, don't drink that, don't chew this, don't smoke that), but it was a new life in Christ, a life of freedom, to be lived under the sunshine of God's grace. To the Romans he wrote: "The kingdom of God does not mean food and drink, but righteousness and peace and joy in the Holy Spirit." [25]

The point I am getting at, Mark, is simply this. Don't let your conscience be tied up by purely human prohibitions which someone has invested with the authority and the sanctity of the divine. Don't let people make a thing a *sin* for you which God Himself has not termed sinful. Above all, don't you yourself blow up matters which are purely "neutral" into matters of heaven-or-hell significance. There is enough of sin in the world without our adding to it by labeling those things sinful which in themselves have no moral implication. *Enjoy yourself,* as God surely wants you to. Free yourself from any taboos or inhibitions which have been self-imposed but which find no warrant in the Holy Scriptures. Remember, the kingdom you have entered is a kingdom of "righteousness and peace and *joy* in the Holy

[24] Colossians 2:13-23 P   [25] Romans 14:17

Spirit." [26] God wants you to have that inner joy which only He can give, and He gives it to all who put their faith in Him and look to Him for guidance.

Perhaps one more thing should be said. Don't keep these "guilt feelings" bottled up within yourself. If they persist, arrange for a heart-to-heart talk with your pastor or with a mature Christian friend in whose spiritual judgment you have confidence. To brood over our feelings of guilt is the surest way to multiply them. To shut them up within our heart is the surest way to drive them deeper and deeper into our consciousness. Bring them out into the light of day, in the presence of your pastor or of a trusted friend.

Remember, Christ has empowered every Christian to speak the word of heavenly pardon in His name. He said: "If you forgive the sins of any, they are forgiven." [27] And on another occasion He said: "Whatever you loose [forgive] on earth shall be loosed [forgiven] in heaven." [28] In the Christian congregation it is normally the called and ordained pastor who speaks the word of divine forgiveness on behalf of the entire congregation and in the name of Christ. Do you remember how Martin Luther explained the above words of the Savior in his Small Catechism? He said: "I believe that when the called ministers of Christ deal with us by His divine command, especially when they . . . absolve those who repent of their sins and are willing to amend, this is as valid and certain, in heaven also, as if Christ, our dear Lord, dealt with us Himself."

One of the main reasons your pastor is there, Mark, is to assure penitent sinners like you and me of God's forgiveness through Christ. How often, on a Sunday morning, have you heard your pastor repeat the well-known words of absolution: "Upon this your confession, I, by virtue of my office, as a called and ordained servant of the Word, announce the grace of God unto all of you, and in the stead and by the command of my Lord Jesus Christ I forgive you all your sins in the name of the Father and of the Son and of the Holy Ghost"? *Those words mean exactly what they say.* They are Christ's words of divine

[26] Romans 14:17   [27] John 20:23
[28] Matthew 18:18

pardon on the lips of His human messenger. If, however, any doubt may linger in your mind, your pastor is there to hear your personal confession in the privacy of his study and to give you the personal assurance that Christ's forgiveness is for *you*. And when he speaks to you of God's love and of His eagerness to forgive whatever you have done, please remember: "this *is* as valid and certain, in heaven also, as if Christ, our dear Lord, dealt with us Himself."

John

*". . . but what if I don't feel God's love . . . what if I don't feel
that I am saved?"*

IX · Anchored in the Rock

Dear Mark:

You have asked a question which has been a matter of deep
concern to many a sincere believer. "What if I don't *feel* that
I am saved?" Many a person who has professed the Christian
faith all his life, and who has made a conscientious attempt to
put his faith into practice, is suddenly filled with deep anxiety
because, for reasons which he cannot explain, he doesn't "feel
saved." Indeed, there are those who, after a lifetime of conscientious Christian living, suddenly feel positively "*un*-saved!"
Does the Bible have anything to say to such people? Does it
have anything to say to you in your present moment of uncertainty? You may be sure, it does.

Let's back away a little from your question for a moment,
so that we can see it in its proper perspective. The Christian
religion, Mark, is based upon a series of historical facts. I know,
of course, that our religion is *more* than history, but it is history
before it is anything else. It is the record of a series of tremendous, unparalleled, and unprecedented acts by which God
entered the stream of human life to rescue a fallen race. You
know the high points of that drama — the birth of the Babe in

Bethlehem, His death on Calvary, His resurrection on Easter morning, His visible ascension into heaven nearly six weeks later, the outpouring of the Holy Spirit on Pentecost, and the miraculous spread of His church as recorded in the Book of Acts and the New Testament epistles. This record was put into writing by eyewitnesses of the events themselves.[1]

The first point I should like to make (and remember, it is only a *first* point) is that our feelings in no way affect the objective truth of these historical events. Feelings do not change history. My feelings about Alexander the Great or Julius Caesar or George Washington or Abraham Lincoln in no way change the historical record. The facts are there, reliably attested by accredited contemporaries. No matter how I may feel about these facts, my feelings will in no way change them. Similarly, no matter how I may feel about the great Biblical drama of redemption — particularly in my darker or more depressed moments — my feelings will in no way erase or even modify the historical record which has come down to us through the centuries. The record will still be there after the clouds of doubt have lifted, and I will wonder why I ever tried to *feel* the glorious record out of existence.

So, too, the interpretation of that record. The same men who wrote the record told us what the record meant. St. Paul put it very clearly when he said: "When the time had fully come, God sent forth His Son, born of a woman, born under the Law, to *redeem* those who were under the Law, so that we might receive the adoption of sons."[2] To the Corinthians he wrote: "God was in Christ, reconciling the world to Himself, not counting their trespasses against them, and entrusting to us the message of reconciliation."[3] St. John, who was closer to Christ that any other man on earth, wrote at length, both in his Gospel and in his First Epistle, about the person and work of the Savior. Christ, he says, is the eternally pre-existent Son of God, who became flesh,[4] who visited this planet for thirty-three years, who died in expiation of human guilt, who rose again, and who now rules in glory.[5] Christ Himself spoke frequently not only of His heavenly origin but also of His heavenly mission. He said:

---

[1] 1 John 1:1-3   [2] Galatians 4:4   [3] 2 Corinthians 5:19
[4] John 1:1-14   [5] 1 John 1:1-3

"The Son of Man came . . . to give His life as a ransom for many." [6] (Jesus applied the title "Son of Man" to Himself no fewer than seventy-eight times in the gospels, frequently to identify Himself as the Messiah-Savior promised in the Old Testament.) Notice, He says: "The Son of Man *came* . . . to give His life as a ransom." You and I don't say that we "came." We say that we were born. Jesus was fully conscious both of His divine origin and of His divine purpose here on earth.

Now, no matter how you or I might *feel* about the meaning which the Bible writers and Jesus Himself give to the great events in the drama of redemption, our feelings can never change their clearly intended meaning. The great events of Christmas, Good Friday, Easter, and Pentecost do not change their significance according to our fluctuating moods and fancies. Regardless of our feelings, Good Friday is still Good Friday — with all of its original meaning. And regardless of our feelings, Easter is still Easter — with its glorious message of assurance. The spiritual significance of these high and holy festivals remains eternally the same.

Now, just as the *fact* of Christ's entry into human history is true regardless of our feelings, and just as the *meaning* of His redemptive work remains true, independent of our subjective reaction to it, so, too, the *method* by which we receive the benefits of His salvation is unchanging and unchangeable. All of us are saved in the same way, and that way is as clear as it is simple. "God so loved the world," said Jesus, "that He gave His only-begotten Son, that whosoever believeth in Him should not perish, but have everlasting life." [7] The key word in that comforting passage, Mark, is "believeth." Again and again Christ spoke of faith, not feeling, as the hand into which God pours all the blessings of salvation. Faith, not feeling, was the watchword of His disciples as they spread the wonderful message of the Gospel from city to city. Paul's entire Letter to the Romans was devoted to *faith* as the hand that reaches up to take the redemption which Christ has won. He writes to the Roman Christians: "Therefore, since we are justified by *faith*, we have peace with God through our Lord Jesus Christ." [8] I repeat, we are saved by faith — not by moods, not by states of mind, not by feelings.

[6] Matthew 20:28   [7] John 3:16 KJ   [8] Romans 5:1

But faith in *what?* Ah, there lies the crux of the problem. To the New Testament writers the answer to that question was self-evident. Why, faith in Christ, of course! Faith in Him as a Person, and faith in what He has done and still does for us, as Savior and Lord. Faith in the "good news" that God, in His mercy, sent His Son into the world in the Person of Jesus Christ, and that through Him we have been redeemed for time and for eternity. The faith that saves us is a faith that is attached to a Person and to a message about that Person. The Person is Jesus Christ, God's Son; and the message is the Gospel of full and free forgiveness through His atoning work. Do you remember what Paul said to the jailer at Philippi? "Believe in the Lord Jesus, and you will be saved." [9] He pointed the jailer to a great Person who was mightily able to rescue him. "Have faith in *Him!*" he said. And let's not forget that when Paul told people to have faith in Christ, he had a very definite kind of faith in mind. He told his Corinthians that they were to put their trust wholly and solely in "Christ, and *Him Crucified*." [10] Not merely the Christ of the Sermon on the Mount, but the Christ of the cross, who died for the sins of the world. That fact — the fact of Christ's death for sinners — was an essential part of Paul's Gospel. Properly understood, it *was* Paul's Gospel. To have faith, in the New Testament sense, means clearly to have faith in a divine Person and in a divine fact. In Christ — and in Him crucified! The New Testament knows of no other "faith" that saves.

Perhaps you've been thinking that I'm belaboring the obvious. By no means! The point I am leading up to is simply this: people who are alarmed about not "feeling saved" usually have made one of two mistakes. Instead of putting their faith in Christ and the marvelous message of redemption through His atoning death, they have either put their faith in their feelings or they have put their faith in faith itself. Instead of putting their faith in something *outside* themselves, they have put their faith in something *inside* themselves, and, believe me, Mark, there is no surer way to agonizing doubt and ultimate despair.

Don't ever put your faith in your feelings. They can change

at any moment. A sleepless night, a rainy day, a case of indigestion, a bad day at the office, trouble at home — any one of a thousand things can change the color of our mood almost before we know it. And the color of our mood has a deceptive way of changing our entire outlook. (I don't mean to seem facetious, but we can feel very much more "saved" after a hearty meal than before — much more "saved" on the day following payday than the day preceding.) And by the same token, don't put your faith in your *faith*. All of us are in danger of looking at our faith as some sort of virtuous thing, as a moral achievement of our own, as something which God has promised (or is obliged?) to reward with the blessing of salvation. When we do that, we are headed for disaster. For we are making of our faith a *work*, a good deed, and we are presuming to stand in the presence of God by virtue of our own accomplishments.

The Bible tells us that no man will ever be able to stand in the presence of God because of his own achievements — not even because of his "faith," if he chooses to point to his faith as something meritorious or as the thing in which he has placed his confidence. Nor shall we be able to stand in the storms of life, when the cruel winds of misfortune all but break the bruised reed of our wavering faith, if all we have to hold on to is "faith." When the storms of life are upon us, we want more than "faith" to cling to. We want Christ! We want His divine assurance!

Does the above sound like a distinction without a difference? By no means. There's all the difference in the world! When the crisis moments of life descend upon us, it will make a tremendous difference whether we have put our confidence in *Christ* or only in our *faith*. Ask the man who has just had a perilous escape from drowning, if there was any difference between the jutting rock to which he clung and his heavy water-soaked clothing. In his moment of despair he did *not* cling to his clothing for rescue — he clung to the rock. He reached *out*, he reached away from himself, and fastened his hand to something infinitely more secure, something unchanging and immovable.

So, too, with you and me, Mark. Sometimes, when we look

inside ourselves for the assurance of our salvation, we fail to
find that assurance. Sometimes, when we search our heart for
just a shred of evidence that we are indeed and in truth God's
children, we fail to find that evidence. We find nothing but the
ugly footprints of our sin. What then? Stop looking inside!
Start looking outside! Look out and away from yourself. Look
to Christ and to the objective assurance of His Gospel. Those
assurances are still there, just as they were there yesterday and
just as they will be there tomorrow. We may have closed the
blinds, but we haven't stopped the sun from shining. Outside
our present darkness, no matter how black it may seem at present, the Sun of Grace is still beaming. God is still in the heavens.
Christ is still on His throne. And every precious Gospel truth
is still as true as on the day He first spoke it. "My sheep hear
My voice, and I know them, and they follow Me, and I give
them eternal life, and they shall never perish, and no one shall
snatch them out of My hand." [11] We may not be able to trust
our own feelings, we may not be able to put confidence in our
own faith, but we *can* trust the One who spoke those words.

The next time you are assailed by gloomy thoughts, especially by gnawing doubts about your soul's salvation, may I suggest that you turn to this page and read these comforting words
by Annie Johnson Flint:

> *I don't look back;* God knows the fruitless efforts,
> The wasted hours, the sinning, the regrets;
> I leave them all with Him who blots the record,
> And mercifully forgives, and then forgets.

> *I don't look forward;* God sees all the future,
> The road that, long or short, will lead me home,
> And He will face with me its every trial
> And bear for me the burdens that may come.

> *I don't look round me;* then would fears assail me,
> So wild the tumult of earth's restless seas;
> So dark the world, so filled with woe and evil.
> So vain the hope of comfort or of ease.

[11] John 10:27

I don't look in; for then I am most wretched;
Myself has naught on which to stay my trust,
Nothing I see save failures and shortcomings,
And weak endeavors crumbling in the dust.

But I look up — into the face of Jesus,
For there my heart can rest, my fears are stilled;
And there is joy, and love, and light for darkness,
And perfect peace, and every hope fulfilled.

Some time ago I heard a young pastor exhorting his congregation in all seriousness and no doubt in all sincerity:"*If* you will put your trust in Christ, He will save you." I believe he used the word "if" five or six times. I have never liked that way of presenting the Christian Gospel. At best, it is misleading. At worst, it can end only in abysmal despair. The Gospel of Christ does not contain an "if" clause. It is a simple declarative sentence. "Christ died for our sins." [12] "God was in Christ, reconciling the world to Himself." [13] In the purest sense, that is the Gospel. It is the announcement of God's love for you and me — in Christ. It is true, we share in the comfort of that announcement only as we believe it, but we shall do well to put our trust in the *announcement itself,* and not in our subjective attitude toward it. The prisoner who has just received word of his pardon by the governor doesn't first ask himself a dozen searching questions like "Do I believe it?" or "Do I believe it with all my heart?" or "Do I have this or that mental reservation?" No, he fastens his entire attention on the oral announcement of the warden or on the official document in his hand. "By order of the governor . . . you have been pardoned. . . ." It is the official *announcement,* bearing the governor's seal, delivered by the trusted hand of the warden, in which he puts his trust. Not in the surge of confused emotions which well up in his thumping heart because of that announcement! You and I, Mark, have received the official announcement of our pardon — the divine covenant of forgiveness, sealed in the blood of Him who loved us.[14] Let us rest our case solely on that covenant.

[12] 1 Corinthians 15:3   [13] 2 Corinthians 5:19
[14] Matthew 26:28

I cannot close this letter without sharing with you my favorite Bible passage on this matter of feeling — or *not* feeling — saved. When the apostle John was a very old man, he wrote to the early Christians, stressing and restressing his favorite theme, the theme of God's love as it had been revealed through the incarnation, life, death, and resurrection of the Savior. To them he wrote: "If our heart condemns us, God is greater than our heart and knoweth all things." [15] I wish you would memorize that passage and tuck it away in your heart for ready and frequent reference. The gray-haired apostle, who in his earlier years had been so close to Christ, had people just like you and me in mind when he wrote it.

There will very likely be days when, despite everything, the "feel" of God's love will seem to have faded from your heart, when the "joy of salvation" will seem a hollow phrase, when your constant failures, your constant sinning, your repeated truancy from the heavenly Father will rise up to accuse you and to rob you of all confidence. It will be at moments like that that the divine assurance of the text above will fall like sweetest music on your soul. Though our heart condemn us a thousand times, though its inner precincts roar and thunder endless accusations, "God is greater than our heart and knoweth all things." The omniscient God knows that we are sinners, but He also knows that in Christ our guilt has been atoned, our sins have been washed away. He knows (what in moments of depression we are prone to forget) that in Christ our sin-stained lives have been accounted righteous in His sight, and that in Christ we shall be more than conquerors.[16]

Therefore, let heart, soul, mind, or whatever other faculty we may have, tell us that we are *lost*. It makes no difference! Our source of assurance rests in His all-knowing love. The anchor of our soul has caught hold of something entirely outside ourselves, it has found its hold in the eternal Rock of Ages. He is "greater than our heart." He knows all things. And it is *He* that tells us we are saved.

There are two lines of an old German hymn which I should

[15] 1 John 3:20 KJ   [16] Romans 8:31–39 KJ

like to commend to you in closing. Memorize them. They hold the answer to your present problem. Translated, they read:

I cling to what my Savior taught,
And trust it, whether felt or not.

Mark, we have a divine Redeemer. In moments of doubt or depression, let us look away from all else, especially from ourselves, and let us fix our eyes on Him.

John

"What if I should die right after I have committed a sin and before I have had an opportunity to ask God for His forgiveness?"

X · Standing in His Grace

Dear Mark:

You ask: "What if I should die right after I have committed a sin and before I have had an opportunity to ask God for His forgiveness?" I need not tell you, of course, that many a person has asked this question before you. It is a very natural question for anyone who takes seriously his moral accountability to God. "What if I should have to step into the presence of a just and holy God with a freshly committed sin on my conscience?"

As natural as this question is, however, it is based on a serious misunderstanding of the Christian Gospel. It would be wrong, Mark, to picture our God as a cruel tyrant who is keeping his eye on us, waiting for us to make the first false move, ready to mete out sudden punishment. It would be equally wrong to picture Him as a mean and humorless book-keeper who is engaged in an endless balancing of our ledger, entering minute-by-minute debits and credits opposite our name — for instance, sixty-seven sins committed on Thursday, sixty-six forgiven on Friday, leaving a balance of one still unrepented and unforgiven!

I know that there are some devout people who are actually

living their lives as though God did operate according to some such system of bookkeeping. In fact, I shall have to admit that in my early years I labored under this delusion. When I left church on a Sunday morning, especially if I had attended the Lord's Supper, I felt that I had a clean slate! Which, of course, I did! But I pictured that slate as being clean only for a fleeting moment. I pictured it as being chalked full of unforgiven sin from the moment I left church until the next time I thought of asking God for His forgiveness! I imagined that slate as being alternately clean and dirty — depending upon how long it was since I last asked God for His forgiveness.

Thank God, Mark, that for you and me that slate is *always* clean! That is the tremendous revelation of the Christian Gospel. We are not the clients of a heavenly bookkeeper. We are the children of a heavenly Father. Through faith in Christ we have stepped *out* of that tit-for-tat relationship with God into which we were born by nature, and by which we could expect nothing else from God but our just deserts. We have stepped into a new relationship in which we can expect nothing but His love, His mercy and compassion. Or to put this marvelous fact into the language of the Scriptures, we have stepped out of the relationship of the Law and into the relationship of grace.[1]

St. Paul writes to his Roman Christians: "Therefore, since we are justified by faith, we have peace with God through our Lord Jesus Christ. Through Him we have obtained access to this grace in which we stand." [2] Those of us who have found forgiveness for our sins in the atonement of the Savior have entered into a brand-new relationship with God, the relationship of grace. ("Grace" in this passage, as in many others, means the unmerited mercy of God.) In this relationship there is no talk of "just deserts," no talk of punishment, no talk of retribution. There is talk only of love, compassion, and forgiveness, of membership in the family of a gracious Father. In this relationship we are, as it were, cradled in the arms of God's omnipotent love every waking and every sleeping hour of our lives. This is the grace — *His* grace — in which we stand.

As long as we are justified by faith, as long as we are stand-

[1] Romans 6:14b   [2] Romans 5:1

ing in His grace, our slate is *always* clean. Do I really mean
that? Most assuredly. Not because you and I haven't sinned,
but because God in His mercy wiped out our transgressions long
ago. He cleaned your slate and mine when His Son visited this
earth and suffered and died and rose again.[3] In Christ's great
act of atonement our slate was wiped clean once and for all
time.[4] In one of my previous letters I wrote at great length of
the tremendous payment which Christ paid for our sins and
how "the blood of Jesus, His Son, cleanses us from all sin." [5]
It is the eternal efficacy of that atonement which keeps our slates
forever clean. That atonement availed for the sins of our youth,
and it will avail for the sins of our old age. It will avail every
moment of our lives, as long as we are living in God's grace.

This is a very important point that I am making. The sin
of weakness which you are going to commit tomorrow, and for
which sudden death may give you no opportunity for repentance,
that sin was forgiven already [6] in God's eternity [7] and was paid
for by an act of divine atonement when God's own Son laid
down His life for you.[8] If I may put it this way, when Christ
died in expiation of human guilt, God handed you and me
a clean slate, a slate which would never again bear the mark
of sin, as long as we are standing in His grace, as long as we
are living under the cleansing power of the blood of His atoning
Son. As Paul puts it, "There is therefore now no condemnation
for those who are in Christ Jesus." [9] The all-important thing,
Mark, is that you and I are "in Christ Jesus." And we *are* in
Him — as long as we put our trust in Him.

There is another passage of Scripture that will bring you
much assurance in this connection. Paul writes to the believers
in Corinth: "God was in Christ, reconciling the world to Himself, not counting their trespasses against them." [10] It is possible
that we have quoted this passage so often and so glibly that we
have never caught its full significance. Read it carefully, and
you will see that the reconciliation of the world to God (another

---

[3] Romans 4:25   [4] Hebrews 7:26, 27
[5] 1 John 1:7   [6] Ephesians 1:3, 4 KJ
[7] 2 Timothy 1:9 KJ   [8] 1 John 2:1, 2
[9] Romans 8:1   [10] 2 Corinthians 5:19

way of saying forgiveness) is something that happened long ago. It was a one-time transaction, completely consummated when Christ died for us. God doesn't have to be reconciled over and over again. He *has* been reconciled! Those who have come to Him through faith in Christ are living in a constant state of reconciliation. Already in eternity-past He decided not to "count their trespasses against them" in view of the atonement of His Son. And so, Mark, that sin of weakness which, despite your best intentions, you are going to commit tomorrow has already been provided for. It is included in that great mass of human transgression that "will not be counted." It was paid for on Calvary more than 1,900 years ago.

Does this sound like an invitation to sin? I shall admit that to many people it does. But right now I am not writing to them. I am writing to *you,* of whom I know that the thought of willful sinning is farthest from your mind. St. Paul realized that the presentation of a Gospel of 100% grace would seem to some to be an open invitation to sin. After pointing out to the Christians at Rome that the forgiveness of their sins was a matter of pure grace, without a shred of merit or worthiness on their part, he asks: "Now what is our response to be? Shall we sin to our heart's content and see how far we can exploit the grace of God? What a ghastly thought! We who have died to sin — how could we live in sin a moment longer?" [11] To Paul and to the other Bible writers it was unthinkable that a Christian would deliberately exploit the grace of God by living in willful sin.

Let's be sure we know the difference between willful sinning and sins of human weakness. The Bible does not say that Christians do not sin. It does not say that a believer who is "standing in God's grace" will never become guilty of serious transgressions. Paul had to admit that, even after he had become a Christian, he sinned — and sinned grievously. [12] Peter, writing to believers, had to tell them what to do about those sins which they committed, even in a state of grace. [13] And the Savior Himself taught His followers to pray, "And forgive us our trespasses." Evidently He knew that even the best of Christians would lapse

[11] Romans 5:20—6:2 P   [12] Romans 7:14-24
[13] 1 Peter 2:1, 2

into sin and be in constant need of pardon. But to the Bible writers, *willful, deliberate* sinning — involving, as it does, a conscious rebellion against the will of God — is incompatible with a life that is being lived "under grace." Conscious, deliberate, willful rebellion against God is a sign that we are not living "under grace."

Far different from such conscious and willful rebellion are the sins of weakness which you and I commit from day to day, the sins to which even Paul had to confess. The sins which, despite our best efforts, we find clinging to us as if glued to our soul. The sins which, almost simultaneous with their doing, fill us with a sense of shame. Some of these may even be great sins, but they are sins to which our "new nature" [14] does not give approval. In fact, we hear its voice of *dis*approval in the very doing of the act. For want of a better name, I am calling these our "sins of weakness," since they stem from the essential weakness of human nature which still adheres even to those who are living in God's grace.[15]

I am sure that it is this type of sin of which you speak when you ask: "What if I should die right after I have committed a sin and before I have had an opportunity to ask God for His forgiveness?" Inasmuch as you would still be a child of God, living in the sunshine of His grace, that final sin of weakness would be drowned with all the rest of your transgressions in the bottomless sea of His mercy, and you would step into His presence washed clean by the blood of the Lamb who died that you might live eternally.

Never forget this one fact: you are standing in His grace. And as long as you are standing in His grace, your slate is clean — every day, every hour, every minute of your life.

John

[14] Colossians 3:10   [15] Romans 7:14-24

"I have prayed again and again, but nothing has ever happened. Does God really answer prayer?"

XI · The Prayer of Faith

Dear Mark:

Does God really answer prayer?

I don't suppose a day passes without having that question asked a thousand times. Frequently, I fear, those who ask it do so because of personal disappointment in their prayer experience. They have wanted something desperately. They have asked God for it — pleadingly, urgently, importunately — but the thing desired was not forthcoming. And so in their perplexity they ask sincerely: Does God really answer prayer? From your letter it is evident that your question has a similar background. You have asked the Lord for something which you have not received, and so you have put a big question mark over the efficacy or the worthwhileness of praying.

Let me begin my answer to your question by posing a question of my own. Do you think God really *wants* you to pray? Do you think He *expects* you to pray? If we can agree that God wants and expects us to pray, I'm sure we can agree that He doesn't expect us to pray for nothing. If it is God's will that His children come to Him with their joys and their sorrows, their problems and their perplexities, surely He has a helpful purpose in mind.

That God wants His children to pray to Him is perfectly clear from Holy Scripture. "Call upon Me in the day of trouble," [1] He tells us in the Old Testament; and "Pray constantly," [2] He tells us in the New. The Savior Himself [3] frequently encouraged His disciples [4] to bring their petitions to God in trusting faith.[5] Perhaps best known of His exhortations to prayer is the familiar passage in Matthew: "Ask, and it will be given you; seek and you will find; knock, and it will be opened to you. For everyone who asks receives, and he who seeks finds, and to him who knocks it will be opened. Or what man of you, if his son asks him for a loaf, will give him a stone? Or if he asks for a fish, will give him a serpent? If you, then, who are evil, know how to give good gifts to your children, how much more will your Father who is in heaven give good things to those who ask Him?" [6] Did you notice the three imperatives with which this familiar passage opens? Ask! Seek! Knock! These are the exhortations of Christ Himself. Surely, there can be no doubt that God *wants* us to pray.

Then, too, think of the vast array of prayer heroes presented to us in the pages of Scripture — presented, let there be no doubt, as examples for us to follow. Abraham prayed. Isaac prayed. Jacob prayed. Moses prayed. Elijah prayed. Elisha prayed. Daniel prayed. David prayed, many of his prayers having been preserved for us in the Book of Psalms. And in the New Testament Peter prayed, Paul prayed, James prayed, the early Christians prayed. In fact, the Book of Acts is in some respects a book of prayers — the prayers of the faithful as they went about the important task of building the church.

The supreme example of a life of prayer, of course, was that of our Lord Himself. According to the Gospel record, He frequently withdrew from the company of others for periods of quiet prayer. For instance, after the miracle of the feeding of the five thousand Matthew tells us that Christ "went up into

---

1 Psalm 50:15   2 1 Thessalonians 5:17
3 Matthew 21:22   4 Mark 11:24
5 John 16:23   6 Matthew 7:7-11

the hills by Himself to pray" and that, when evening came, He was still in the hills "alone." [7] Luke tells us that on the evening before Christ chose His twelve apostles He "went out into the hills to pray," and that "all night He continued in prayer to God." [8] In the seventeenth chapter of his Gospel John has recorded the imperishable words of Christ's great intercessory prayer,[9] the prayer which He addressed to His Father in behalf of those from whom He was soon to be separated by death at the early age of thirty-three. And who will ever forget the example of pleading and persistent (albeit, humble and submissive) prayer which the Savior gave us in the Garden of Gethsemane on the night before His crucifixion? "My Father, if it be possible, let this cup pass from Me; nevertheless not as I will, but as Thou wilt." [10]

In view of the explicit commands of Scripture that we pray, and in view of the vast array of heroes of prayer which cross its pages, but above all, in view of the example of our divine Lord Himself, can there be any doubt, Mark, that God expects us to pray? And if He expects us to pray, can there be any doubt that He attaches a helpful and a salutary purpose to our prayers? Indeed, the Scriptures are filled with His promises to *answer* our prayers. The Old Testament "Call upon Me in the day of trouble" is followed by the divine pledge "I will deliver you." [11] And the New Testament "Ask" is followed by the divine assurance "It will be given you." [12] If there is one thing the Bible makes perfectly clear, it is that the Lord not only expects us to pray but that He also *expects us* to *expect Him* to answer.

Look, for a moment, at these reassuring passages of Holy Scripture, all related to the subject of prayer. David, the shepherd boy who became king and who in his adult years literally prayed his heart out, writes in one of his psalms: "The Lord is near to all who call upon Him, to all who call upon Him in truth. He fulfills the desire of all who fear Him, He also hears their cry and saves them." [13] The Lord says through the Prophet Isaiah: "Before they call I will answer, while they are yet speak-

7 Matthew 14:23   8 Luke 6:12
9 John 17:1-26   10 Matthew 26:39
11 Psalm 50:15   12 Matthew 7:7
13 Psalm 145:18

ing I will hear." [14] Jesus says to His disciples: "Therefore I tell you, whatever you ask in prayer, believe that you receive it, and you will." [15] On another occasion He tells them: "Truly, truly, I say to you, if you ask anything of the Father, He will give it to you in My name." [16] The aged apostle John writes toward the close of his life: "We have such confidence in Him that we are certain that He hears every request that is made in accord with His own plan. And since we know that He invariably gives His attention to our prayers, whatever they are about, we can be quite sure that our prayers will be answered." [17] Surely, anyone who accepts the Bible as his authority in spiritual matters must believe that God not only hears but also answers prayer.

I realize that these blanket statements still leave many questions unanswered. What about those prayers for quiet and refreshing slumber which are followed by seemingly endless hours of restless sleeplessness? What about those prayers for confidence, poise, and self-assurance which are followed day after day by the same flock of butterflies, buckling knees, and sweaty palms? What about those prayers for health which are followed by sickness, those prayers for domestic tranquillity which are followed by domestic strife, those prayers for death which are followed by months of pain on a bed of "hopeless" illness, those prayers for refreshing rain which are followed by parching drouth, those unnumbered prayers in which we plead with God to say "yes" but to which His answer seems to be a monotonous, heartless "no"?

Let me be perfectly frank with you, Mark, and say that I, too, as a fallible and finite human, have frequently experienced great difficulty in trying to reconcile the sweeping promises of Scripture with those individual instances where the fervent prayers of Christians have seemed to go unanswered. I am sure, however, that my difficulty (as yours, too) stems from the very fact that I *am* fallible and finite. I am not God. I am not omniscient. At no given moment in my earthly journey can I see my *whole* life in its full perspective, and so at no point am I in a position to sit in judgment on the acts of God, as

---

[14] Isaiah 64:24　　　[15] Mark 11:24
[16] John 16:23　　　[17] 1 John 5:14, 15 P

He shapes and guides my destiny. He alone can see the end from the beginning, and so He alone can know with infallible certainty what to do with my prayers as they ascend to His throne of grace. Here I must bow in humble and trusting submission to His Word: "My thoughts are not your thoughts, neither are your ways My ways, says the Lord. For as the heavens are higher than the earth, so are My ways higher than your ways and My thoughts than your thoughts." [18]

But I need not bow like a dumb dog before its master. I can rather yield to His will as a trusting child yields to the will of a loving father. Remember, the God to whom you and I pray is not some inscrutable Providence away out yonder in the far reaches of the universe; He is the *"Our Father"* to whom our Savior told us to direct our prayers. And as our Father, He is going to handle all of our prayers, not only according to His superior wisdom but also according to His proved love.

I mention His *proved* love. That is one fact which we shall have to pin down again and again, if we are to cope successfully with the problem of "unanswered" prayer. As a believer in Christ, you know that God loves you. The whole Gospel of redemption, including, as it does, the incarnation of God's Son, His death in your behalf, His resurrection, His ascension, and His continued intercession for you at the throne of His Father — all of this is an unmistakable revelation of God's love for you. God no longer has to prove His love for you; He has done that once and for all time in the redemption He has wrought for you through Jesus Christ, His Son. In view of this tremendous demonstration of God's love, the apostle Paul exclaims in the well-known passage which I have quoted previously in our correspondence: "What then shall we say to this? If God is for us, who is against us? He who did not spare His own Son but gave Him up for us all, *will He not also give us all things with Him?"* [19]

If you will read that passage in its setting, you will see that Paul was speaking of the Christian life in the context of eternity, as a life predestined by God "before the foundation of the world," to be lived with Him in glory long after this world has crumbled into dust.[20] That is how you and I will have to look

---

[18] Isaiah 55:8, 9   [19] Romans 8:31, 32   [20] Romans 8:28-39

at our lives, if we are to approach this business of prayer as the Scriptures would have us approach it. We are to view our lives as being written, from beginning to end, by a pen which is held in the hand of divine Love. A loving Father in heaven has already read the final chapter of your life, a chapter of unspeakable bliss and glory, and He is seeing to it that the chapters which are being written today fit into the story plot. All you and I need to know for sure is that the pen which is doing the writing is in the hand of Love. And that we know! God has assured us of that through the incarnation of His Son and through His death in our behalf.[21]

It is in view of the above assurance that Paul asks the rhetorical question: "Will He not also give us all things with Him?" What did Paul mean by "all things"? Surely not all things in the absolute sense. Not the Empire State Building. Not an all-expense-paid round trip to Hawaii. Not a controlling share of the stock of U. S. Steel. To the ultimate attainment of God's good and gracious purpose in our lives, these things may be no more important than rubbish. But He *will* give us "all things" that are necessary to accomplish those spiritual and eternal purposes which He has set for us. He *will* give us "all things" that are necessary to insure our ultimate enjoyment of His presence throughout the endless ages. That is the meaning of this marvelous eighth chapter of Romans.

But what about those specific requests to God for things which are evidently good, but which go unfulfilled? Don't they give the lie to such promises as "Ask, and it will be given you"? I shall have to admit that, on the surface, there does seem to be a contradiction. But the contradiction is only on the surface. Whenever we are confronted with apparent contradictions of this kind, it will pay us to remember the rule that "Scripture interprets Scripture." Sometimes it is necessary to bring the light of Scripture as a whole to bear upon an individual passage before we can understand it fully. It is true, Jesus told His disciples: "Truly, truly, I say to you, if you ask anything of the Father, He will give it to you in My name." [22] But it is also true that this same Jesus, on the night before His crucifixion, pleaded with His heavenly Father that He might be spared the agonies of the following day. Yet He was not spared. Did His prayer go unanswered? Did the "prayer promise" He had given His disciples prove false or valueless at this crucial moment? The same Man who had told His followers that, if they had faith the size of a mustard seed, they could move mountains,[23] was unable to stop Roman soldiers from nailing Him to a cross. Where was *His* faith at that moment?

The apostle Paul, who encouraged the early Christians to be constant in prayer [24] and who himself was a man of fervent prayer,[25] was not ashamed to admit that certain of his petitions went "unanswered." Repeatedly he pleaded with the Lord to remove a certain affliction from him (his "thorn in the flesh"), but, as far as we know, Paul carried his affliction with him to his grave.[26] It is evident, then, that the Bible does not consider Christian prayer as a sort of heavenly cash register, whose keys we need only press — and, presto, the money-filled drawer swings open! The Bible does not present prayer as something mechanical or automatic. Above all, it does not present prayer as a device by which we can subordinate God's will to ours, or by which we can subject His will to our whim. Evidently there are prayers, sincere prayers, which God chooses to answer with a fatherly "no," or which He chooses to answer in a manner entirely different from that which we have indicated in our petitions.

The Scriptures themselves give us the key to this particular aspect of prayer. We find it in the First Epistle of St. John. There we read: "We have such confidence in Him that we are certain that He hears every request that is made *in accord with His own plan*." [27] The significant phrase in this passage is "in accord with His own plan." The Greek word which Phillips translates "plan" literally means "will." In the sense that God has a well-defined *will* for your life and for mine, the word can also mean a plan or design. Therefore we might paraphrase this passage: "We have complete confidence in God and are

---

[23] Matthew 17:21   [24] Romans 12:12

[25] Acts 9:11   [26] 2 Corinthians 12:7-9

[27] 1 John 5:14 P

certain that He hears and answers every request which we address to Him and which is in conformity with the plan which He Himself has determined for our lives." This qualification or limitation might be discouraging and distressing if you and I did not already know that His plan for you and me is a plan of grace, designed for our eternal good.

It is this qualification ("in accord with His own plan") which explains why the great apostle, despite his repeated prayers, had to carry his thorn in the flesh with him to the grave. God had a "plan" for Paul, and millions of Christians down through the centuries have endorsed the love and wisdom which lay behind that plan. It is this qualification, too, which explains why the Son of God Himself, after groveling in prayer in the dust of Gethsemane, had to rise from prayer and walk directly into the hands of His captors — to be bruised, beaten, insulted, spit upon, and finally nailed to a cruel cross. God had a "plan" for His Son, and millions of Christians down through the centuries have endorsed the love and wisdom which lay behind that plan. Indeed, Mark, you and I might well learn to pray all of our petitions for earthly blessings, if not in the language, then at least in the spirit of Gethsemane: "Nevertheless not as I will, but as Thou wilt." [28] Not my petty designs of the moment, but Thy *grand* design, Thy gracious and eternal purpose, be accomplished in my life.

There are some gifts for which we can ask without qualification. Not because we deserve them more than others, but because, with respect to them, God has revealed His will to us. When we *know* God's will, we need not say, "If it be Thy will." We know that it is His will to forgive our sins, to cleanse our souls from guilt,[29] and to preserve us blameless in His sight until the Day of His heavenly kingdom.[30] With respect to these blessings, the blessings of the soul, we can come before Him with complete confidence, knowing that He will grant us our petition. Here we need not say: "*If* it be Thy will." We can say: "*Since* it is Thy will." That is the glory of the Christian religion. It has revealed to us the gracious will of God to forgive, to sus-

[28] Matthew 26:39   [29] Romans 8:28-39
[30] 2 Timothy 1:12

tain, and to preserve the souls of those who put their trust in Jesus Christ, His Son. There is no "if" about His ultimate purpose of love, and so there need be no "if" in our approach to Him for the blessings of pardon, peace, assurance, and final spiritual victory.

But there are many areas of life in which His will for us is not as yet revealed. Is it His will, for instance, that I continue in good health and that my life be extended another twenty years? I have no way of knowing. Is it His will that I continue in my present work next year — and the next? That I purchase the home I looked at yesterday? That I drive my old car another year? That I take that vacation I've been promising myself for, lo, these many months? That the jet plane which I shall take next week will arrive safely at the airport in Los Angeles? God has given us no specific revelation of His will in matters such as these, and so when we bring them to Him in prayer (as, indeed, we should),[31] we should present our petitions subject to His will: "Lord, if it be Thy will. . . ." And let there be no mistake about it: if His will should not agree with ours, He will bless us in the very withholding of our requests! We shall be the better, not only for having asked but also for having been denied — for we shall have acknowledged, lovingly, the supremacy of His will and the goodness of His "plan."

Sometimes I think we fail to thank God sufficiently for all of our "unanswered" prayers. Think what might have happened to our lives if the omniscient God of heaven had overruled His own omniscience instead of our ignorance, and had granted us everything we asked for, and in the *way* we asked it! What a shambles we might have made of our lives! How much better that His love and wisdom prevailed! How often, from the perspective of later years, have we been able to look back and repeat the convictions of the unknown poet —

> I asked for grace to lift me high
> Above the world's depressing cares;
> God sent me sorrows — with a sigh
> I said, "He has not heard my prayers."

[31] Philippians 4:6

I asked for light, that I might see
My path along life's thorny road;
But clouds and darkness shadowed me
When I expected light from God.

I asked for peace, that I might rest
To think my sacred duties o'er.
When, lo! such horrors filled my breast
As I had never felt before.

"And, oh," I cried, "can this be prayer
Whose plaints the steadfast mountains move?
Can this be Heaven's prevailing care?
And, O my God, is this Thy love?"

But soon I found that sorrow, worn
As Duty's garment, strength supplies,
And out of darkness meekly borne
Unto the righteous light doth rise.

And soon I found that fears which stirred
My startled soul God's will to do,
On me more lasting peace conferred
Than in life's calm I ever knew.

Let there be no doubt about it, Mark: whenever you address your Father in heaven, through Jesus Christ, your Lord, your heavenly Father hears your prayer. Indeed, He knows the secret and unspoken wishes of your heart.[32] If these are in accord with His own plan for you, He will grant them in due time. If they are not, He will grant you something very much better. Remember, the Scriptures tell us that God is "able to do far more abundantly than all that we ask or think." [33] All He asks is that you come to Him in trusting prayer — "as a dear child to a dear father" — and that you leave the final "yes" or "no" entirely up to Him, knowing confidently that *His* will is always better than your own.

John

[32] Psalm 19:14   [33] Ephesians 3:20

"Could it be that God is punishing me now for a terrible sin which I committed in my youth?"

XII · Chastened But Not Punished

Dear Mark:

I am sure that many an adult Christian has been troubled, at one time or another, with the haunting thought that he is being punished for some specific misdeed of his youth. Especially is he exposed to this kind of thinking when, after life has run smoothly for a number of years, he is suddenly confronted by a series of reverses. Family strife, wayward children, a broken home, financial difficulties, disillusionment, protracted illness — these and a dozen similar personal tragedies can provide fertile soil for the seeds of real or imagined guilt to take root and flourish.

Could it be that God is finally balancing my account? That He is giving me exactly what I deserve? That my sins at last have found me out? To be specific: that sin of impurity committed in my early youth — could God be punishing me for *that* by giving me such wayward children? That sin of dishonesty committed shortly after I established my business some twenty years ago — could God be punishing me for *that* by sending me my present financial reverses? Those sins of pride and arrogance, of ingratitude and indifference, of hypocrisy and insincerity, of hatred and bitterness, of religious lukewarmness and spiritual neglect which characterized my early years — could God be punishing me for *those* by confining me to this bed of illness? And if He is, how long shall I have to suffer my punishment? When will my punishment be paid?

Just to put those questions black on white is enough to show you, Mark, how utterly incompatible they are with the God whom you and I have learned to know through Jesus Christ. The God whom you and I have learned to know and trust is the God of infinite love and pity and compassion. Can you imagine the God of the Christian Gospel carrying a grudge or a "score to settle" against one of His redeemed? Can you imagine His forgiving "but not *forgetting*" the sins of those who have come to Him in penitence and faith, pleading the merits of His Son?

The Scriptures assure us: "I will forgive their iniquity, and I will remember their sin no more." [1] That promise of God stands sure. Incomprehensible though it may be to us, God's ability to forget is as perfect as His ability to remember — and, as far as your sins are concerned, He has promised to forget! Those sins that you have brought to Him in your private prayers, your public confession at church, and in your uncounted little conversations with Him throughout the day — those sins He has long since thrown into the infinite sea of His "forgetfulness." You, too, can say, as did King Hezekiah: "Thou hast cast all my sins behind Thy back." [2] And you may be sure that any sin that has been cast behind the back of the Almighty is going to remain exactly where He cast it.

In one of my previous letters to you I quoted from Psalm 103, a psalm of David. Perhaps I should quote it again. Remember that David in his old age had committed some terrible sins to which he could look back, including the sins of adultery and murder. Remember, too, that David in his later years was called upon to experience heartbreaking trials and tribulations,[3] such as it is unlikely that you and I shall have to endure. Yet David maintained his faith in God's immutable promise to forgive and to forget, both the sins of his youth and those of his old age.

---

[1] Jeremiah 31:34   [2] Isaiah 38:17   [3] 2 Samuel 18:33

Listen to him as he becomes lyrical in his praise of God's never-ending mercy:

> The Lord is merciful and gracious,
> slow to anger and abounding in steadfast love.
> He will not always chide,
> nor will He keep His anger forever.
> He does not deal with us according to our sins,
> nor requite us according to our iniquities.
> For as the heavens are high above the earth,
> so great is His steadfast love toward those who fear Him;
> As far as the east is from the west,
> so far does He remove our transgressions from us.
> As a father pities his children,
> so the Lord pities those who fear Him.
> For He knows our frame;
> He remembers that we are dust.[4]

Did you notice the significant lines? "He does not deal with us according to our sins, nor requite us [pay us back] according to our iniquities." He has thrown the record book away. He is no longer keeping account. There are no longer any scores to settle, no longer any debts to pay. There is nothing that we have done that He intends to "pay back." And then look at that other sentence: "As far as the east is from the west, so far does He remove our transgressions from us." Our sins are not kept in a folder in His top drawer, handy for ready reference at some strategic moment; they have been removed as far as the east is from the west. To David, that was a poetic expression for infinity. The infinite God has taken your sins and mine and removed them so far that they shall never again rise up against us and successfully accuse us.

I need hardly remind you why this is possible. This is possible, Mark, because your sins and mine have *already* been punished in the Person of Jesus Christ, God's Son. As I have pointed out in previous letters, everything that needed to be done to clear your record, to clean your slate, was done when Jesus died for you. It is as simple as that. If this sounds too simple, remember that it was this very *simplicity* of the Gospel which Paul pointed

[4] Psalm 103:8-14

out as its greatest glory and which he was constantly at great pains to defend.[5] I don't know which sin of your past has been troubling you, but I do know that Christ died for it,[6] that He paid for it,[7] that He suffered its punishment,[8] and that, because He did, our Father in heaven has forever erased it from His memory.[9] If He is willing to forget (and He assures us that He is!), I am sure He does not expect us to torture ourselves by insisting on remembering.

If we were to believe that God still punishes those who have come to Him through Jesus Christ, we would be forced to one of two impossible conclusions: either the atonement which Christ has made for our sins was not complete, or God the Father is exacting *double* payment for our iniquities. Both conclusions are both unscriptural and unthinkable.

The Bible tells us that Christ's atonement was perfect and complete. God has been reconciled to us — not only 50%, not only 90%, not even only 99%, but 100%. The blood of Jesus Christ, God's Son, has cleansed us from *"all sin."*[10] I have always found great comfort in the fact that the Bible uses the singular "sin" here and not the plural "sins." Had the plural been used, there may have been a lingering doubt (unfounded, of course) as to one specific sin in a certain city some forty years ago. But by using the singular "sin" the Bible has lumped all of our iniquity into one total ugly mess and told us that God has washed the entire business down the drain. We have been washed clean from sin — from sin in bulk!

The Epistle to the Hebrews goes to great pains to impress the fact that the redeeming work of Christ was perfect and complete. His one great act of atonement left nothing for us to atone. According to this epistle, the Old Testament priests had to offer their sacrifices again and again in symbolical payment for the sins of the people, but the great High Priest, Jesus Christ, brought only one sacrifice in which He paid "once and for all time" for the entire sin-account of the entire human race. The writer closes this particular section of his epistle with the significant statement: "Where God grants remission of sin, there can be no ques-

---

5 1 Corinthians 1:18-31   6 Isaiah 53:4, 5   7 Romans 8:1
8 2 Corinthians 5:19-21   9 1 John 1:7—2:2   10 1 John 1:7

tion of making further atonement." [11] The Scriptural argument is simply this: Were God to punish you today for something you did, say, twenty years ago, He would be exacting a *second* punishment, since His Son already atoned for that sin when He gave His life in expiation on the cross.

No, Mark, since you have entered into a grace-relationship with God, based on the complete atonement of His Son, there can be no talk of "punishment" for the sins of your past. There can be talk only of forgiveness, forgiveness which is complete, comprehensive, all-inclusive; forgiveness which is free and undeserved, the unmerited gift of His mercy. God's attitude toward you can be none other than that of love. It can be neither vindictive nor punitive. Through Christ He has become your Father, and you have become His child. In this filial relationship all talk of punishment or retribution is unthinkable. To you and to me and to all who have returned to the bosom of the Father through the mediation of the Son, He says: "I have loved thee with an everlasting love; therefore with loving-kindness have I drawn thee." [12] "Behold, I have graven you on the palms of My hands." [13] "Fear not, for I am with you; be not dismayed, for I am your God; I will strengthen you, I will help you, I will uphold you with My victorious right hand." [14] In this new relationship of grace God is always *for* you, never *against* you.[15] Whatever He sends you has found its point of origin in His fatherly affection.

But what about those unpleasant dispensations which even devout believers receive from the hand of God — financial ruin, social rejection, physical incapacity, sickness, pain, untimely and unexplained bereavement, plus that long list of personal tragedies to which very few of us are strangers? Are these not punishments sent from God? By no means! If they were punishments, they would issue from God's holiness, His justice, His wrath upon our disobedience. But the Bible tells us that, in the case of believers, these unpleasant visitations issue solely from His love. They are not punishments, but chastenings. Not the expression of His anger, but the expression of His fatherly affection. They are

[11] Hebrews 10:18 P   [12] Jeremiah 31:3 KJ   [13] Isaiah 49:16
[14] Isaiah 41:10   [15] Romans 8:31

part of that gracious discipline which, in an adverse world, is necessary to bring us closer to His loving heart and to keep us in the firm grip of His guiding and sustaining hand.

Again and again the Bible speaks of the adversities of the believer as a part of a heavenly discipline, motivated by the Father's love and designed for the believer's good. Let me quote a substantial section from the Epistle to the Hebrews which deals with this very thought. (The indented quotation which this New Testament writer reproduces is taken from the Old Testament Book of Proverbs). I shall quote from J. B. Phillips' paraphrase. The writer to the Hebrews says:

"You have perhaps lost sight of that piece of advice which reminds you of your sonship in God:

> 'My son, regard not lightly the chastening of the Lord,
> Nor faint when thou art reproved of Him;
> For whom the Lord loveth He chasteneth,
> And scourgeth every son whom He receiveth.'

"Bear what you have to bear as 'chastening' — as God's dealing with you as sons. No true son ever grows up uncorrected by his father. . . . After all, when we were children, we had fathers who corrected us, and we respected them for it. Can we not much more readily submit to a heavenly Father's discipline and learn how to live?

"For our fathers used to correct us according to their own ideas during the brief days of childhood. But God corrects us all our days for our own benefit, to teach us holiness.

"Now obviously no 'chastening' seems pleasant at the time: it is in fact most unpleasant. Yet when it is all over, we can see that it has quietly produced the fruit of real goodness in the characters of those who have accepted it in the right spirit. So take a fresh grip on life and brace your trembling limbs. Don't wander away from the path but forge steadily onward. On the right path the limping foot recovers strength and does not collapse." [16]

To the writer of the above epistle, as well as to all other Bible writers, there is a big difference between being *punished*

[16] Hebrews 12:4-13 P

by God and being *chastened* by God. It is the same difference as exists between a rebellious hoodlum being bludgeoned by a police officer and a devoted child being disciplined by his father. The police officer is acting in the name of the law and is meting out justice for the sake of justice. The father is acting in love and is offering correction for the good of the child. Both as to motivation and objective, the policeman and the father are as far apart as possible. And certainly the hoodlum and the devoted child are also as far apart as possible — in the spirit in which they accept the proffered "correction." The hoodlum knows only that he is being bludgeoned; the son knows that he is being built.[17]

And so I come back to the question in your letter which occasioned my reply tonight: "Could it be that God is punishing me for a terrible sin which I committed in my youth?" And I answer categorically, "No, it couldn't." The God who has forgiven you in Christ has forgiven you all the way. His thoughts toward you are only thoughts of love. If you are undergoing some unusual trial, please be sure it is not a sign of His wrath or anger. It is rather an indication of His fatherly concern. It is your good, both temporal and eternal, that He has in mind. Remember the words of Christ? He pictured His Father as a Vinedresser who is interested in every vine and every branch in the vineyard. "Every branch that *does* bear fruit He prunes, that it may bear *more* fruit."[18] Although at the moment you can see only the sharpened blade of the pruning hook, you can be sure that the Vinedresser is preparing one of His fruitful branches for an even greater yield. Just what the fruit is that He has in mind, you and I cannot tell at present. We do know that the fruit of the Spirit is "love, joy, peace, patience, kindness, goodness, faithfulness, gentleness."[19] We know, too, that "suffering produces endurance, and endurance produces character, and character produces hope, and hope does not disappoint us, because God's love has been poured into our hearts through the Holy Spirit which has been given to us."[20]

Of one thing you can be sure. The present trial will pass and, in God's gracious providence, you will be the better for it.

John

[17] Romans 5:3-5   [18] John 15:2
[19] Galatians 5:22   [20] Romans 5:3

"I find it so hard to read the Bible. When I do read it, there is so much in it that is hard to understand, and some of the things I do understand are so hard to believe."

XIII · There's Treasure in the Word

Dear Mark:

Recently I received a letter from a devout woman who was in great spiritual distress, verging on despair. She had been a life-long member of the church, had been regular in her prayers and church attendance, had been active in the church's program and, in general, had done most of those things which are expected of good church members. There was one thing she had failed to do ever since coming into the church as a child by the rite of confirmation, and that was to read her Bible regularly.

She was now in her fifties and was determined to make up for this neglect. She began to read her Bible every evening. But to her shock and dismay she "just couldn't stay with it." Again and again she tried, but the book "just seemed a jumble of words." She began with Matthew and got midway through the epistles when she finally gave up in despair. A less devout or less sensitive person might have soon forgotten it, but this good woman could not pass it off and could not forget. In fact, she began to "feel guilty through and through" and was "ashamed to admit to the pastor or to my friends that I couldn't read through half a chapter without getting completely lost." What troubled her most and prompted her to write was the accusing question: "Does this mean there's something wrong with *me?* Am I too wrapped up in the things of this world to become interested in the things of God? Could it be that I am not spiritual enough to grasp what the Bible means? Could it be that I am not one of Christ's followers after all?"

Needless to say, my heart went out to this woman, as it does to all who have shared in her unfortunate experience. For let there be no mistake about it, this woman is not alone. She is only one of many spiritually sensitive people who are harboring a sense of secret guilt because they are unable to read their Bibles enjoyably and intelligently and are afraid or ashamed to admit it. I am going to say something right here, Mark, that may surprise you; but I must say it if I want to be honest and if I want to relieve your mind of the burden which (I sense) you bear. I sincerely believe that there has been much talk about Bible reading during recent years that was both sentimental and irresponsible. In some cases, I fear, good church members who were both unsuspecting and unprepared have been coaxed, cajoled, shamed, pressured, and "programed" into Bible reading — on the grounds that the Bible is an easy book to read. That simply is not true!

In fact, the Bible is a *difficult* book to read. How could it be anything else? It was written by men who lived thousands of years ago in a section of the world whose geography, customs, culture, and civilization were entirely different from our own. Against their own background, utterly foreign to anything we have ever seen or experienced, these men wrote in their own languages — languages which are no longer spoken. These languages had to be laboriously translated into English before the average person could read what they had written. How can we expect such a book to be "simple reading" for the housewife, the clerk, the mechanic, or the merchantman who was born thousands of years later on a distant continent and in a civilization which is completely out of touch with the one in which the book was written? Of all the writers I have read, I have found none more difficult than St. Paul — not only because of the depth of his subject matter but also because of his disconcertingly unorthodox methods of composition and his terribly involved syntax.

The church will succeed only in producing confused and "guilt"-ridden members if it pursues a consistently sentimental approach to this matter of Bible reading. Whether or not the historical books of the Old Testament or the epistles of the New Testament were meant to be read "devotionally" by the housewife or in the average family circle will, for me at least, remain a debatable question; of one thing I am sure, they are not "easy." And the church should admit this openly and frankly, lest it add to the anxieties of those sensitive members who, having been thoroughly frightened by their first encounter with the open Book, have begun to doubt — either the Book or themselves!

In saying the above, I am not claiming that the Bible is not a clear book as far as the *way of salvation* is concerned, or as far as those doctrines are concerned which are necessary for Christian faith and life. The deity of our Savior, His sacrificial death for sinners, salvation by grace alone through faith, the precious sacraments of Holy Baptism and the Lord's Supper, the fellowship of the Christian church, the return of Christ to Judgment, the eternal bliss of the believers, these and all those other doctrines on which our Christian hope is based stand out crystal clear in the pages of Holy Writ. Any child in the upper grades of grammar school can read and understand the passages which deal specifically with these basic doctrines. To say that, is one thing. It is an entirely different thing to say that the Bible as a whole is an easy book to read, or that it can be picked up and read enjoyably at leisure just like any other book. It is when we say, or even *imply,* the latter, that we open the door to anxiety for many a tender soul. For many a tender soul has found that, at least in his case, the Bible cannot be read that way.

I have written the above somewhat at length, Mark, because I have reason to suspect that you are one of those tender souls. I wanted you to know that the fact that you are having difficulty in your Bible reading in no way casts a shadow on your faith in Christ as Savior or on the sincerity or validity of your Christian faith in general. You need have no guilt feelings here. On the other hand, I would not want you to let down in your efforts to become more and more familiar with the Scriptures. It is in the Scriptures ultimately that we find the Christ who is the "chief

Cornerstone" of our faith. We will therefore not want to neglect them. May I make a suggestion? For the time being, at least, I would suggest that you look upon your Bible as a book to be *studied* more than as a book to be *read* — as a book to be approached *studiously* more than a book to be approached *casually* or *leisurely*. Later on, perhaps, you can reverse these emphases. But right now you will do well to face up to the necessity of the hard approach.

If you are not a member of a Bible class, I would urge that you join one. The guidance of a trained instructor and the stimulation of fellow searchers will mean very much to you. Buy a few of the modern translations of the Bible which come closer to our contemporary idiom. You will notice that in my correspondence with you I have quoted from three versions, the Revised Standard, the King James, and the paraphrases of J. B. Phillips. I would strongly recommend especially the last named for the lay reader. Don't try to get along without a Bible dictionary and a few commentaries. You will find these almost indispensable. The point that I am making is simply this: if you have come to a standstill in your Bible *reading*, turn, with even greater diligence than before, to Bible *study*. You may well find that in your case this is the only way you can handle the Scriptures effectively.

Now let me go on to the other comment in your recent letter. You say: "When I *do* read my Bible, there is so much in it that is hard to understand, and some of the things I do understand are so hard to believe." Here, too, I am sure that your experience is shared by many. As for certain sections of the Bible being hard to understand, let me give you the "comfort" of knowing that even the most learned theologians have found certain passages of Scripture extremely difficult to explain. Some years ago a United States Senator was eating in a Pullman diner, enjoying a dinner of fish. The young man seated opposite him had noticed that, while waiting for the waiter to serve him, the Senator had read from a small pocket Bible. Curious, the young man opened up a friendly conversation: "Sir, I noticed that you were reading a Bible. I, too, used to read the Bible, but I finally gave it up." "I'm sorry to hear that," replied the Senator. "And why, may I ask, did you stop reading it?" "There were too many things

I couldn't understand, too many unanswered questions, too many things for which I couldn't find a rational solution." After a momentary pause the young man continued: "Tell me, Sir, what do *you* make of all the Bible difficulties?" The Senator thought a moment, then pointed to a little pile of fish bones near the outer edge of his plate. "I treat them like those bones. I find plenty of meat in the Bible, and when I come across a bone that I can't handle, I just lay it aside."

Might I suggest that, for a while at least, you just follow the example of the Senator? There is plenty of meat in the Bible for you to eat a long time without becoming involved with the bones. Difficult passages? Yes, there are many of them in the Bible. But we do not turn to *those* passages when our faith is weak, our spirits low, and our heart is in need of reassurance. The hungry man does not turn to the bones for sustenance, he turns to the meat. And, by the same token, the man who is spiritually insecure should not turn to the Bible's *difficulties* to feed his faith; he should turn to its crystal-clear promises. And the Bible is full of those!

Some time ago a distressed church member wrote to me, saying that he was in agonizing doubt as to his own soul's salvation, not because of some horrible crime he had committed but because he was no longer sure in his own mind concerning certain Scriptural statements, most of them in the Old Testament. What I wrote to this troubled man may also prove helpful to you. I suggested that he learn to regard God's revelation to us in the Scriptures as a series of concentric circles. Into the very center of His revelation to us God has placed His Son, Jesus Christ. In the circles immediately surrounding this center He has revealed to us those doctrines which relate to His Son and to our eternal salvation. As the circles go out from the center and become ever larger, they include other revelations, equally divine in their origin, but not essential to our salvation.

I suggested that in moments of doubt or depression he always hurry back to the center — and stay there! Go to the Christ! The Christ of the Bible, to be sure. Not to the Christ of our own imaginings. In terms of the written Word, this means go back to the transparently clear and sublimely simple statements of the Savior Himself: "I came that they may have life, and have it abundantly. I am the Good Shepherd. The Good Shepherd lays down His life for the sheep." [1] "My sheep hear My voice, and I know them, and they follow Me; and I give them eternal life, and they shall never perish, and no one shall snatch them out of My hand." [2] "The Son of Man came to seek and to save the lost." [3] "The Son of Man came . . . to give His life as a ransom for many." [4] "Come to Me, all who labor and are heavy-laden, and I will give you rest." [5] "For God so loved the world that He gave His only-begotten Son, that whosoever believeth in Him should not perish but have everlasting life." [6] These are the words of Christ Himself. Until the storm of doubt blows over, I suggest that the troubled soul stand right here — with his eyes on the Son of God Himself and his heart open to His invitation. Soon all doubt, misgiving, and foreboding will melt in the sunshine of His smile.

When the clouds have lifted, we can again venture boldly into the next circle of God's revelation, then the next, and then the next. But we will always remember that it is in Christ, the heart and center of God's revelation to us, that we have found salvation. To that center we can always return when the storms begin to blow and the wick of faith burns low. The man who remembers this will not be thrown into an agony of terror or will not see the jaws of hell opening up for him every time he runs into a "Bible difficulty" out in the peripheral areas of Christian revelation. By saying this, Mark, I am not saying that some parts of Scripture are more inspired or more authoritative than others; I am rather saying that, when it comes to answering the agonizing cry of the tortured soul, some passages of Scripture must naturally take precedence. These are the passages which present to our wondering view the Christ, the Christ of the cross, the Christ of the outstretched arms and open hands, the Christ who says to you and to me: "Come!" [7]

May I suggest that you keep this counsel in mind every time

[1] John 10:10, 11   [2] John 10:27, 28
[3] Luke 19:10   [4] Matthew 20:28
[5] Matthew 11:28   [6] John 3:16 KJ
[7] Matthew 11:28

you approach your Bible either to read it or to study it, or as you meditate upon it throughout the day? There will always be some passages which baffle you, there may even be some which trouble you and give rise to spiritual doubt. But let none of these take from you that Pearl of Great Price which God has tucked snugly and securely into the very center of His revelation — His Son who died for you and rose again!

John

"I feel so inadequate. Especially when I'm in the company of others, I become painfully aware of how inferior I really am."

XIV · Children of the Father

Dear Mark:

Some time ago I was having an interesting conversation with a competent psychiatrist who, in addition to being an outstanding man in his profession, is a fine Christian gentleman. How is it, I asked him, that people who have no religious convictions whatever frequently display a resoluteness and self-confidence which are the envy of everyone around them, while the deeply religious person is often overcome by a sense of his own inadequacy and stands timidly by while the door of opportunity closes in his face? Or, to put it more simply, why is it that the non-religious person frequently has a healthy, glowing sense of *sufficiency*, while the devout person frequently is immobilized by a paralyzing sense of *insufficiency?*

My psychiatrist friend lost no time in replying. In fact, his reply came so fast that I got the feeling I had touched upon a subject which had become a "sore spot" with him. "Because the religious person has taken the virtue of humility and made a disease out of it!" he blurted. I shall never forget that answer. I am passing it along to you tonight in partial reply to your no doubt sincere complaint: "I feel so inadequate!"

No one will deny that humility is a Christian virtue, but even humility can become a sickness if we permit it to. We can drive this business of humility to such an extreme that ultimately the only service we can render to society is that of doormats — and surely our confused and wicked world today has a right to look to the Christian community for more than doormats. The prophet Micah had some pertinent words to say in this connection:

> He has showed you, O man, what is good;
> and what does the Lord require of you
> but to do justice, and to love kindness,
> and to walk humbly with your God? [1]

To the prophet Micah the devout man was the man who could walk erect among his fellows, his head high, his shoulders back, doing justice and loving kindness, while at the same time walking humbly, with bowed head, in the presence of his God. There is surely nothing contradictory in the idea of walking erect among our fellow men and at the same time walking with bowed head in the presence of our God. The big danger for you and me, Mark, is that, as believers, we have become so obsessed with our own littleness, our own nothingness, in the sight of God that we carry this obsession over into our relationships with our fellow man. We have become so accustomed to acknowledge our unworthiness in God's sight — in our prayers, our hymns, our worship service — that, without realizing it, we develop what might be called an "unworthiness complex" in all relationships of life. No matter what the challenge, we have convinced ourselves that we are inadequate to meet it. We are too small, too weak, our talents too limited. This, I agree with my psychiatrist friend, is not humility. It is a disease.

It would be impossible, of course, to do justice to this subject within the brief scope of a letter. Feelings of inadequacy may have many roots, and in cases where these roots run deep it would take the skillful efforts of a competent psychiatrist to uncover and untangle them. I doubt, however, that such is your case. At any rate, let me point out a few theological considerations which may put you on the road to greater confidence and greater self-assurance.

[1] Micah 6:8

If there is anyone in the world who should *not* be despondent or depressed by feelings of inadequacy, it is the believer in Christ. And why not? (I hope that my answer is not going to sound too abstract or too abstruse. The fact is, my answer is not at all abstract. It is more real and more relevant than anything else anyone might say in this connection. The difficulty lies in our failure to make daily contact with this reality.) The reason the Christian should be the last person in the world to succumb to feelings of inadequacy is *his awareness of who he is.* Did you ever stop to think, Mark, of the exalted dignity with which the Lord has invested the individual believer? St. John in the opening chapter of his Gospel makes a remarkable statement, a statement which becomes more tremendous in its implications every time I read it. He is speaking of the miraculous coming of Christ into the world; and into this lofty passage he inserts the following thought almost parenthetically: "As many as received Him, to them gave He power to become *the sons of God,* even to them which believe on His name: which were born, not of blood, nor of the will of the flesh, nor of the will of man, *but of God.*" [2]

"The sons of God — born not of the flesh — but of God!" That is who you and I are. If our religion means anything to us at all, it must mean exactly what those words imply. God has reached down into the stream of humanity and has picked you and me out of the mass of humankind and has placed on us the royal robes of sonship. We are the sons of God, not merely in the generally accepted meaning that we are His creatures, but in the infinitely more sublime sense that He has redeemed us by His blood, has made us members of His family, and has "raised us up with Christ and made us sit with Him in the heavenly places." [3] Nor are we merely "sons of God." We are "*the* sons of God," the ones whom He has chosen to wear the ring of sonship secured by the death of His Beloved. This is the theme of the entire New Testament. "Behold, what manner of love the Father hath bestowed upon us," St. John writes toward the close of his life, "that we should be called the sons of God!" And in the next verse he continues: "Beloved, now are we the sons of

[2] John 1:12, 13 KJ   [3] Ephesians 2:6

God, and it doeth not yet appear what we shall be; but we know that when He shall appear, we shall be like Him, for we shall see Him as He is." [4] Sons of God today who, when He comes again, shall be "like Him." Such is the high dignity with which God invests all who are His through faith.

Someday I should like to make a study of all the titles which the Bible ascribes to the individual believer in Christ — salt, light, saint, chosen, elect, redeemed, beloved, child of God, king, priest — and then I should like to contrast these titles with the timid, craven, apologetic, and defeated attitude some of us have fallen into. God has not called us His slaves — He has called us His *sons*, "heirs of God and fellow heirs with Christ." [5] St. Peter tells the believers, and that means you and me: "You are a chosen race, a royal priesthood, a holy nation, *God's own people,* that you may declare the wonderful deeds of Him who called you out of darkness into His marvelous light." [6]

Now I know what you are thinking. Reciting Bible passages isn't going to help me when I'm in the presence of people to whom I feel decidedly inferior, or when I'm confronted by a task for which I feel entirely inadequate. You are right, Mark. Reciting Bible passages *is not* going to help. At least, not in the way your objection indicates. The prize fighter does not become a strong man because of the meal he ate a few hours before ring time; he became a strong man because of the thousands of meals he ate before his first engagement and because of the exercise and discipline which enabled him to convert those meals into physical strength and energy. If you and I are to learn to face life assured and unafraid, adequate to the challenge of each new day, we shall have to feed our minds on the daily remembrance of who we are. Not mice, but men! And not only men, but sons of God, ransomed and redeemed, and sent into God's workaday world to serve. We shall have to remember morning, noon, and night that we wear the royal robes of sonship and that He who is our Father is the omnipotent and omnipresent God of heaven. To every son who puts his trust in Him, the Father says:

[4] 1 John 3:1, 2 KJ   [5] Romans 8:17
[6] 1 Peter 2:9

Fear not, for I am with you,
be not dismayed, for I am your God;
I will strengthen you, I will help you,
I will uphold you with My victorious right hand.[7]

There is another basic Bible teaching which we should bear in mind in this connection. God has given each of us a "gift" which is to be used for the common good. None of us has been overlooked. This is how St. Paul put it: "Men have different gifts, but it is the same Spirit who gives them. There are different ways of serving God, but it is the same Lord who is served. God works through different men in different ways, but it is the same God who achieves His purposes through them all. Each man is given his gift by the Spirit that he may make the most of it."[8] Now, it is true that Paul was speaking here of spiritual gifts, but what he says of spiritual gifts is true of other gifts as well: the endowments of personality, intelligence, and specialized arts and skills. All are God-given, and all have been given, as Paul says, to serve "the common good."

The point here, Mark, is that you and I have each been given our own particular gift, and whatever that gift may be, it is important in the achievement of God's plan. It is up to us to find out what our particular gift is and then to go all out in using that gift for God's glory. Nor should we feel at all inferior, if our own particular gift is less spectacular than that of someone else. I'm sure you remember how Paul describes the Christian church as the body of Christ, with each believer a member of that body. There would be no point, he says, in the foot being jealous of the hand or of the ear being jealous of the eye, or of any member being judged inferior or superior to another. All are important to the proper functioning of the whole, and all stand in equal honor before God.

In a similar sense this interdependence of gifts applies to all relationships of life. I am by profession a writer. If the mechanic at the gas station down the street were standing next to my typewriter right now, he would very probably feel uncomfortably "inferior." Tomorrow morning when I stop at his

[7] Isaiah 41:10   [8] 1 Corinthians 12:4-7 P

station for gas and he begins to talk about that jumble of metal under the hood of my car, I, too, will feel uncomfortably "inferior." But how foolish! Instead of either of us feeling inferior to the other, I should thank God that there are some men in this world who are mechanics, and he should thank God that there are some men in this world who are writers. Is there any reason why the ear should be jealous of the eye? No, both should thank God that he has made one an ear and the other an eye, so that both can contribute to the common good.[9]

Remember, Mark, that this same principle applies to you whenever you are in the company of those people to whom you feel "so inferior." Very probably some of them feel the very same way toward you. God has given you a gift which some of them have not received. It may not be a spectacular gift, but it is a gift of God, a gift which He has been using for the good of others. It may be the gift of a pleasant personality, a pleasing smile, the gift of sympathetic understanding, the gift of empathy which draws the less fortunate toward you for comforting encouragement. It may be any one of a thousand different gifts, but you *do have it,* and God is using it, and those around you are benefiting from it. Your gift may not be one of those that claim the spotlight. It may be one of those that make their greatest contribution unnoticed, unseen, and unheard; but if you have been using the gift which God has given you to the best of your ability, you have no reason to feel "inferior." What is more, if your friends are as intelligent and as high-minded as you, I am sure that they have never thought of themselves as being superior to you.

There is no surer way of making ourselves miserable than by dwelling unduly on the "superior" gifts of our friends in such a way that we are constantly downgrading our own. If you know a friend who is extraordinarily gifted, thank God for the gifts He has given your friend. And let your friend know that you *do* thank God for his good fortune. Such open, willing, and grateful acknowledgment will go a long way toward dispelling any thought of jealousy or self-pity. But while you thank God for the gifts He has given your friend, don't forget to thank Him

[9] 1 Corinthians 12:12-31

for the gifts He has given *you*. A truly grateful heart will never feel inferior.

I notice that in your letter you not only use the word "inferior"; you also use the word "inadequate." Let me assure you, Mark, I know what you mean by that word "inadequate." It is a dreadful thought — this thought of not measuring up to life. Of not measuring up to what the Lord has a right to expect of us. But let me assure you, too, that in many instances this thought is completely without foundation in fact. I have reason to believe that, despite your fears, you are "measuring up" much better than you think.

There is a doctrine in the Bible which, for want of a better designation, I shall call the divine principle of *unequal expectation*. This principle comes into play in God's dealings with each of us. He does not expect the same performance (quantity-wise) from each of His children. He expects more from some than He does from others. Do you remember the Savior's parable of the talents? [10] In a way, it is unfortunate that the parable has that name, since the word talent today has an entirely different meaning. In the parable a talent was a weight of silver or gold, worth approximately $1,000. Today a talent is a natural gift or endowment. But let us look at the parable and then see how it applies to your personal feelings of inadequacy.

As Jesus told the story, the headman of the house gave each of his servants a different amount of money with which they were to deal until he would return. To one he gave $5,000, to another $2,000, and to another $1,000. When he returned, the first servant had increased his $5,000 to $10,000, the second had increased his $2,000 to $4,000, but the third hadn't done a thing with his $1,000. He had simply gone to sleep on the job. And so he returned his $1,000 just as he had received it. Jesus then speaks in great detail of how the headman commended the first two servants but condemned the third.

There are at least three points in this parable which I should like to highlight. First, each servant was given an opportunity, a challenge for which he was going to be held responsible. Sec-

[10] Matthew 25:14-30

ondly, each servant was given his opportunity or challenge "according to his own ability," that is, according to his own divinely given capacity to handle it. And thirdly, the headman expected only a proportionate performance from each of his servants. Now let's take a brief look at those three points.

First, each servant was given a definite challenge. His measure of silver or gold was his challenge. For you and me, Mark, that challenge is the open door of opportunity which greets us at the dawn of each new day. It is the challenge to make a constructive contribution to the total good of all mankind by means of our particular gifts as we apply them in our particular calling. To the conscientious homemaker, the daily challenge is that of being the best possible wife and mother. To the craftsman who is devoted to his trade, the daily challenge is that of putting the best possible workmanship into a product in which he can take pride. To the faithful worker in the factory, the daily challenge is that of putting in a day of honest work for which his conscience will commend him when he lays his tools aside. To each, the daily challenge is to pursue the course of his vocation in a way which will bring a maximum of glory to his Maker and a maximum of good to his fellow man. (I used the Latin word "vocation." Normally I prefer the English word "calling," since it is easier to hear the voice of God in it.)

Secondly, the challenges which the headman put before his servants and of which he expected them to make the most, were proportioned to their individual capacities to handle them. "To each according to his ability," the Savior says. The headman did not give each servant $5,000, nor did he give each $1,000. He gave one $5,000, the other $2,000, and the other $1,000. Why? Because he was personally acquainted with his servants and knew that they were not all endowed with the same abilities. The $1,000 man was not equipped to face the $5,000 challenge, but he *was* equipped to handle the $1,000.

Similarly, God, "who knows our hearts," presents us with only such authentic challenges as are commensurate with the abilities He has given us. These are the challenges and opportunities which we meet in the daily pursuit of our calling, be our calling that of a bank president, a shoe salesman, a bricklayer, a handyman, or housewife. Whatever our station in life, whatever our calling, whatever our peculiar endowments of body, mind, and spirit, God knows them, and He will confront us with only such challenges as are proportionate to these abilities.

Thirdly, and this is the point of the parable which is especially pertinent, the headman expected only a proportionate performance from each of his servants. Quantitywise, he did not expect the same amount from each. He was glad when the $2,000 man increased his sum to $4,000 and did not chide him for not having matched the $10,000 of the more highly endowed servant. Similarly, Christ tells us that God Himself has a divine principle of *unequal expectation*. Not all of us have the same natural endowments to start with, and not all of us are given the same opportunities. And so God does not expect the same quantitative performance from all of us. He expects our performances to vary greatly. In only one respect does He expect our performances to be equal: we should all be faithful.

Sometimes, I fear, the conscientious Christian is overwhelmed by a sense of his own inadequacy not so much because he underestimates his own ability as because he *overestimates* what God expects of him. He feels "inadequate" not so much because he underestimates his natural endowments as because he *overestimates* the size of the "talent," the measure of gold which God has placed into his hands and which He expects him to bring back doubled. If we have an exaggerated conception of the role in life which God expects us to play, it is inevitable that we shall finally give way to feelings of inadequacy. God did not expect every Indian to be a chief, nor does He expect every soldier to be a general. If we have built up our role out of all proportion to what might be considered our normal station in life, the thing for us to do is to reassess our own appraisal of our role.

I don't know whether the above is true in your case, Mark, but if you think there is a possibility that it is, may I suggest that you give this matter some serious thought. Perhaps a heart-to-heart talk with a trusted friend or with a respected colleague will help you determine the exact size of your talent — the role in life which can reasonably be considered yours. Make the whole matter a subject of daily prayer. Open your heart to God — humbly, frankly, trustingly. If you have been overestimating what God expects of you, if in your own mind you have built up your role in life beyond all reasonable proportion to your normal station, you can pray God for the courage and the grace to make the necessary adjustments. When we find that our shoes are too big, there is only one thing to do: get smaller ones.

Of one thing you can be sure: If you are pursuing a calling into which the Lord has placed you, no matter how high or how low, the Lord Himself will give you the adequacy to meet the challenge of each new day. The apostle Paul once said: "Not that we are sufficient of ourselves to claim anything as coming from ourselves; our sufficiency is from God." [11] And so is *yours,* Mark. Whatever adequacy you possess is from Him, and you may rest assured that He will match your abilities to the role in life which He has chosen for you. May I suggest the following as an appropriate morning prayer each morning before you leave for work:

Grant Thou me strength to do
With ready heart and willing,
Whate'er Thou shalt command,
My calling here fulfilling;
To do it when I ought,
With all my might, and bless
The work I thus have wrought,
For Thou must give success.

With this prayer in your heart you will be adequate to meet the challenge of the day.

John

[11] 2 Corinthians 3:5

"I go to church every Sunday, but I just can't keep my mind on the service. Please don't just tell me to 'keep my mind on it.' That's what I've tried for thirty years — but it just won't work. Is there something wrong with me?"

XV · In Spirit and in Truth

Dear Mark:

In one of your recent letters you spoke at some length and with no little alarm about your inability to keep your mind on the service when you go to church. I shall be honest with you. I have intentionally delayed my answer to that particular letter because I was uncertain as to how to reply. There were two courses open to me. I could give you the conventional stock suggestions, those usually given in sermons or in books on formal worship, and let it go at that. From tragic experience, however, I know that such advice *could* serve merely to deepen your anxiety, since it may completely overlook the real problem which confronts you. On the other hand, I could give you a few suggestions which in all probability would come closer to your problem, but the implementation of which may call for more independent and courageous action than you had bargained for. I have decided to give you *both* sets of answers and to let you decide which comes closer to solving your particular problem.

The preparation for a satisfying worship experience on Sunday morning really begins on the previous Monday. If we are to get the most out of our approach to God and His approach to us during that brief period of formal worship every Sunday, we shall have to live close to God throughout the week. This means not only a life which is consistent with our Christian profession as we live it at the office or the shop, on the streetcar or the bus, at the party or at the social get-together, but also as we live it in our family circle and in our personal inner life. I know this doesn't apply to you, Mark, but I have known people who have lived unspiritual lives from Monday morning until well after Saturday midnight and then have wondered why they found it difficult to get in tune with the Sunday morning service. Some have even blamed their inattentiveness and boredom on the pastor. Why doesn't he deliver more interesting sermons? The family or the individual who lives from Monday until Saturday as though God were a million light-years distant will frequently find Him just as far away while they doze in their pews on Sunday morning.

A satisfying worship experience on Sunday morning calls for worship throughout the week! It calls for personal and family prayers as an integral part of the daily routine. It calls for personal and family devotions — a family altar. It calls for fathers and mothers speaking to their children about the things of God throughout the week. In order to get the most out of our worship on Sunday mornings, we shall have to live home lives which are God-related, Christ-related, and church-related. In that way the Sunday worship will be but an extension of our worship throughout the week. If, by any chance, you have fallen down in one or the other of these requirements, may I suggest, Mark, that you have a talk with your pastor and ask him to recommend a few books which will help you and your family cultivate a more worship-filled home life. I am sure you will find it will pay rich dividends.

Especially important for a satisfying worship experience on Sunday morning is the spiritual preparation on Saturday evening. I know of a Christian father who every Saturday at the supper table reads the Gospel and the Epistle for the following day and explains them to the family. In fact, this is being done in more family circles than you may think. And you may be sure that fathers who take seriously their duty to prepare their families for worship are themselves the better prepared for having done so.

Much depends, too, on our attitude during the moments immediately preceding the service. What has become the usual "last-minute rush" with many families is surely not conducive to effective worship. I would suggest that you try to get to church a few minutes early and that you use those minutes for quiet, thoughtful, prayerful preparation. The prayer of David may well be a model for you during these quiet moments: "Let the words of my mouth and the meditation of my heart be acceptable in Thy sight, O Lord, my Strength and my Redeemer."[1] In addition to some set, formal prayer, I would suggest that you make a practice of using your own words, imploring the Lord that He bless your worship.

You and I belong to a liturgical church, and it is therefore highly important that we spare no effort to become thoroughly acquainted with the liturgy and the significance of each of its parts. I would suggest that, if you haven't done so, you make a serious and conscientious study of all the component parts of the Order of Morning Service, the Order of Matins, and the Order of Vespers. I am sure that your pastor has ample literature on these orders of service and that he would be more than happy not only to lend you a book or two but also to discuss them with you at his leisure.

Of one thing we must be sure. Before we say that we cannot keep our mind on the service, we must be able to say — before God, and with all good conscience — that we have done everything in our power to *keep* our mind on it. We must be sure that our trouble is not simply due to inertia, laziness, or mental or spiritual lassitude. Above all, we must be sure that our failure to keep our mind on the service is not willful. Some people simply make up their minds that they cannot follow the service and then, no matter how much additional light they may receive, they stick to their decision not to follow it. To repeat, whatever our reasons for not being able to keep our mind on the service, we must be sure that they can stand before God.

[1] Psalm 19:14 KJ

It is because I sincerely believe that there *are* such reasons that I am now proceeding to the second part of my letter. I am fully convinced that, for some people, many of the suggestions I have made thus far could lead only to deeper anxiety and to stronger feelings of guilt. Knowing you as I do, and remembering the almost emotional tone with which you wrote of your problem, I have a feeling that you may be one of those for whom the above suggestions, good and valid as they are, could possibly lead only to more frustration. Do you remember what you wrote? I'll repeat your words: "I go to church every Sunday, but I just can't keep my mind on the service. Please don't just tell me to 'keep my mind on it.' That's what I've tried for thirty years — but it just won't work. Is there something wrong with me?" I'm going to surprise you, Mark. In a sense, I'm coming over to your side. I am *NOT* going to tell you simply to "keep your mind on it." Because, all circumstances considered, perhaps you can't.

It is just possible that the fault is not with you, but with a form of worship for which you are both mentally and temperamentally unsuited. I know that that is a dangerous statement to make, but I have been around too long to doubt its essential validity. I am convinced, beyond the faintest shadow of doubt, that not every man is temperamentally suited for liturgical worship. C. S. Lewis, a Christian layman whose devotion is beyond question, admits in his autobiography, *Surprised by Joy*, that he never succeeded in developing a taste for the liturgical service and that he was temperamentally unsuited to participate in *any* formal rite or ritual. I am sure that he is only one of many.

After all, the manner and the method of our public worship is a matter of human choice; it has no divine command behind it. If we have done our very best to conform to the human pattern and find that, despite our most conscientious effort, the pattern is not a suitable vehicle for our worship, we should experience no feelings of guilt. The Lord has not made us all alike, and it would be too much to expect that any set form of worship could be followed with equal profit by all types and conditions of men. I am sure that if all of us could choose our denominational affiliation solely on the basis of public worship patterns, there would be a tremendous fruit-basket upset. There would no doubt be a large-scale exodus from the liturgical denominations to the nonliturgical and perhaps a considerable exodus also in the opposite direction.

Remember, I am not saying that one type of service is good and the other bad. I am merely saying that no one should feel guilty or suffer anxiety because he finds it impossible to fit comfortably into the pattern. The pattern is a purely human device. Nor need you feel any sense of discomfort at your inability to be "educated" to a full appreciation of a given form of worship. The idea that all men are equally educable in the field of liturgical appreciation or in the art of public worship through set patterns is entirely without basis. As well contend that all men are equally educable in the appreciation of art and music.

What I am trying to do, Mark, is to relieve your conscience of any sense of guilt over your inability to "keep your mind on the service," *if* that inability is due to your innate inability to conform to the human pattern. There are some things that some minds simply cannot do, and the Lord is not going to hold you responsible for your inability to keep your mind on a form of worship which is purely the arrangement of fallible men.

Let no one burden your conscience by telling you that such an attitude betrays an irreverence or a lack of appreciation for the Word of God. Indeed, it may be just the opposite. I am thoroughly convinced that in many instances it is the man whose conscience has been sensitized to the majesty of the Word who is the most seriously disturbed by his inability to "keep his mind" on the service. He cannot endure anything less than a whole-souled and whole-minded approach to Word and Sacrament, and so he is overcome by an increasing sense of guilt every time he finds his mind occupied even partly in the trappings. No, Mark, I do not believe that your attitude betrays any irreverence. I think it reveals a healthy respect for the Gospel and for everything sacred.

But what to do?

If, as is possible, your inability to keep your mind on the service is due to a mental and/or temperamental maladjustment to your congregation's set form of worship, I would again suggest a heart-to-heart talk with your pastor. Perhaps there are others in your congregation who feel the same way. Perhaps there are others who *should* feel the same way, but are not spiritually awake enough to feel one way or the other. If a majority share your feelings, there is no reason in the world why your congregation should not change its order of public worship to suit the majority of its enlightened membership. In all probability the changes would not have to be major, and they could be effected without disturbing good order.

But what if you find that you are the only one who has experienced this problem — or one of a small minority? I would suggest, then, that you pray the Lord for a double measure of His grace and that, with His help, you do everything possible to worship Him wholeheartedly through the set forms your congregation now is using. I know that I am telling you to do something which you have conscientiously tried to do for thirty years without success. But I do wish that you would try once more.

And what if you fail?

The Lord Jesus once had a long discussion with a Samaritan woman by the well at Sychar. Among other things they discussed the matter of true worship. What Jesus said on that occasion still holds true for you and me. They had begun (we might say) to "argue" technicalities in the proprieties of worship, but Jesus decided to brush all technicalities aside and come right to the point. He said: "The hour cometh, and now is, when the true worshipers shall worship the Father in spirit and in truth; for the Father seeketh such to worship Him. God is a Spirit, and they that worship Him must worship Him in spirit and in truth." [2] I have always felt that when Jesus spoke those words, He spoke them with no little animation — characteristic of millions of subsequent discussions of this question down through the centuries. You will notice that in His eagerness He uses the phrase "in

[2] John 4:23, 24 KJ

spirit and in truth" two times in close succession. No doubt He wanted to underscore them heavily.

Let me underscore them heavily for *you*. Whatever you do in church on Sundays, make sure that you are worshiping the Lord of heaven in spirit and in truth. That is, with the noblest powers of your mind as they attach themselves to the *true Reality*, which is God. There may be sections of the liturgy which for you are barren and unprofitable. For instance, I believe you mentioned that you simply cannot endure a chant and that your mind gets "all mixed up at the very thought of a responsive reading." Well and good. Let the chant go by and skip the responsive reading, but the meanwhile fix your heart and mind and soul on the God whom you have come to worship. It is He that counts, not the offending chant. There may be stretches in the liturgy with which your mind will never mesh. (I think that is true of many of us.) Use those stretches the more firmly to fasten your thoughts on the eternal God of your salvation. Face up to the fact that for you there will always be holes in the order of public worship, but determine to fill those holes with lofty thoughts of Him who died for you and rose again that you might live. You will notice, I am not telling you here to do something which the years have proved you cannot do; I am suggesting that you do something *new:* that you frankly accept your incompatibility with the morning service and approach the problem creatively, constructively.

I trust that in this letter I have done at least three things: pointed you to ways of getting more out of the present service than you have been getting; absolved you of any sense of guilt if you are one of that large number who, despite their most conscientious efforts, cannot stay with a liturgical service uninterruptedly from beginning to end; and suggested a way by which you can come to terms with an order of service for which you have very little taste without doing injury to your conscience. I pray that, in some little way, I have been of help.

John

"I can't get any rhyme or reason out of life. Everything seems so aimless, so purposeless, so completely mixed up. Can there really be an intelligent plan or design behind it all?"

XVI · The Pattern He Has Planned

Dear Mark:

Have you ever found yourself all confused, looking at a road map, unable to make head or tail out of it, and then suddenly noticing that you hadn't opened it completely? There was still another flap to be unfolded, and it was on *that* section of the map that many of the tangled and twisted highways finally converged. Once you unfolded the final flap, everything began to make sense.

It's very much the same with your life and mine.

Any man who tries to get rhyme and reason out of human existence, while confining his perspective to the few short years between his birth and death, is bound to come up with little rhyme and far less reason. He is working with a map which hasn't been completely unfolded, and too many of the criss-crossed highways seem to end up nowhere. The fact is, as you and I well know, that human existence doesn't end with death. There's another flap which will have to be unfolded before the pattern is completed.

You can be sure, Mark, I fully understand the thinking behind your question: "Can there really be an intelligent plan or design behind it all?" If ever there was a time when human life seemed to make little sense (I mean that part of it which lies between the signing of our birth certificate and the filing of our death certificate), that time is now. For every question modern man has answered he has raised a dozen for which he has no answer. He is, as it were, surrounded by a labyrinth of dead-end streets, roads that lead to nowhere. Unless he can find an authoritative road map of human existence which is fully opened — including the flap on which all the devious highways of his life are destined to converge — his deepest and most searching questions will go begging for an answer.

But God has given you the answers, Mark. At least enough of them to let you know that there *is* a pattern and that the pattern is in His hand. God wants you to view your life not by a perspective which is limited by human birth on the one end and human death on the other, but by a perspective which on the left has you and God in eternity past and on the right has you and God in eternity future. (Strictly speaking, there can be no "eternity past" or "eternity future." Time and eternity do not mesh. I am using these terms merely as an accommodation to the limitations of our human mind.)

The fact is that God had you in His mind already in eternity past, and He wants to have you at His side throughout eternity future. Birth and death are mere incidents in God's completed plan for you. Until you unfold those two flaps — the one on the left, before your birth, and the one on the right, after your death — you are not going to get much rhyme or reason out of the tangled lines that lie between. You can thank God that He has revealed just enough of what is on those flaps to put your mind at ease.

Before the world began, God determined to send His Son to this planet of ours, not merely to redeem mankind in general, but to redeem *you in particular*, so that you could live with Him after the world itself had ended. You were the object of His concern long before He put the sun, the moon, and the stars in their places. And He wants to keep you the object of His concern long after the sun, the moon, and the stars will be gone forever. The Bible tells us that before you and I ever saw the light of day, God determined to bring us into eternal fellowship with Him. It says: "*Before time began,* He planned to give us, in Christ, the grace to achieve this purpose. . . . For Christ has completely abolished death and has now, through the Gospel, opened to us men the shining possibilities of the life that is eternal." [1] And in another place the Bible speaks of "everlasting life which God, who cannot lie, promised before the beginning of time." [2]

That is the first point you'll have to pin down if you ever want to get rhyme and reason out of human life, particularly *your* life. God thought of you (*you,* Mark, the very person who is reading this letter) before He rolled the sun into its present course. Before He studded the summer sky with myriads of stars, He plotted a course by which He could bring you into eternal fellowship with Him. He decided not only to save your soul through the miracle of the cross but also, through His Holy Spirit, to bring you to a saving faith in your Redeemer. That is where you stand right now.

And the second point which you will have to pin down is this. The plan which God has charted for your life is not going to end in a cemetery. Just as that plan had its origin in an eternity which lies behind us, so it will have its complete fulfillment in an eternity which lies before us. We'll never *begin* to understand His ways with us until we realize there's a flap which has not yet been unfolded, and we'll never *fully* understand His ways until He Himself unfolds the final page.

Presumptuous as it may sound, only the man who has come to know Jesus Christ as the Son of God and Savior of his soul can ever hope fully to get rhyme and reason out of living. Only the man who can see God loving him in eternity past, who can see Christ redeeming him in eternity present, and who can see God welcoming him into blissful fellowship with Him throughout eternity future, can fit the jigsaw pieces of his life into a pattern that is meaningful and purposeful. That, in fact, is the Christian Gospel. The Bible says: "Whatever we may

[1] 2 Timothy 1:9, 10 P   [2] Titus 1:2 P

have to go through now is less than nothing compared with the magnificent future God has planned for us. The whole creation is on tiptoe to see the wonderful sight of the sons of God coming into their own." [3] And in another place it says: "These little troubles, which are really so transitory, are winning for us a permanent, glorious, and solid reward out of all proportion to our pain." [4] Perhaps clearest and most reassuring of all are those classic words in the Epistle to the Romans: "To those who love God, who are called according to His plan, everything that happens fits into a pattern for good." [5]

Now what does all of this mean to you and me, especially on those days when our lives seem a crazy jumble and when nothing that happens to us seems to make sense? It can mean very much, Mark. In fact, it can mean everything. It can mean the difference between deep and dark despair or bright refreshing hope. The person who has put his eternal destiny into the hands of God through faith in Christ can have the divinely wrought assurance that, no matter how tangled the skein of his life may seem, the threads are in the hands of a loving Father; and in the hands of a loving Father they are bound to have a loving purpose in the pattern He has planned. I do not know who wrote the following poem, but whoever it was had surely learned the secret of letting God make sense out of our lives.

> My life is but a weaving
> Between my Lord and me;
> I cannot choose the colors
> He worketh steadily.
> Ofttimes He weaveth sorrow,
> And I in foolish pride
> Forget He sees the "upper"
> And I the "under" side.
>
> Not till the loom is silent
> And the shuttles cease to fly,
> Shall God unroll the canvas
> And explain the reason why

3 Romans 8:18, 19 P   4 2 Corinthians 4:17 P
5 Romans 8:28 P

> The dark threads are as needful
> In the weaver's skillful hand
> As the threads of gold and silver
> In the pattern HE has planned.

May I suggest, Mark, that you remember the Christian assurance of this poem on those days when you feel that your life is, as you say, "so aimless, so purposeless, so completely mixed up." God has assured you that there *is* an intelligent plan behind your life, even though at this moment it may be impossible to see it. For a complete explanation of some of the painful sideroads and twisted byways of our life we may have to wait until the final flap of the map has been unfolded — the flap which brings us ultimately to the city of our God. But, at least, we know there is still another page, and we know that God Himself has promised that when the final page has been unfolded, it will vindicate His wisdom and His love.

John

*"I am giving considerably more than a tithe of my income to
church and charity, but when I hear or read of the great need
throughout the world, I begin to accuse myself for not giving
more. I feel so guilty. How can I ever know when I've
done my duty?"*

XVII · Stewards of God's Blessings

Dear Mark:

Some time ago, in one of my letters to you, I made the statement
that the believer in Christ knows of inner conflicts of which the
insensitive worldling has never even *dreamed.* There can be no
doubt that the whole question of Christian stewardship involves
just such a conflict. It is a conflict completely outside the
experience of the worldling — a conflict reserved, as it were, for
the spiritually enlightened. For instance, can you imagine the
materially-minded man tossing in his bed at night because of
his anxious concern for the spiritual plight of the heathen in
New Guinea? Can you imagine him experiencing any sense of
guilt when his alcohol bill for the month exceeds his contributions to the physically and spiritually destitute of Hong Kong,
Korea, or the Near East? Can you imagine him the tortured
victim of anxiety when his losses at the races exceed the monthly
check he has instructed his secretary to send to his favorite
charity? We might just as well expect a corpse to feel ill at

ease over the expensiveness of his own funeral as expect a non-spiritual man to experience any serious anxiety over his personal malfeasance in the field of stewardship. I am using the word "stewardship," of course, in the conventional sense in which you and I have become accustomed to using it: our personal account-ability to God, through Jesus Christ our Savior, for the use to which we put His various gifts to us, both spiritual and material.

I know that in your present frame of mind it will be small comfort, indeed, for me to say that your anxious thoughts in this connection are an unmistakable pulse beat, indicating the presence of the Spirit of God who is at work in your heart. But I shall say it nevertheless. It is because I am convinced that I am writing to a man in whose heart the Spirit of God is truly and effectively at work, that I can make bold to write the following paragraphs as I intend to write them. Believe me, there are some people to whom the following paragraphs should not be written. They are the nonspiritual, who have never come into a relationship of grace with God and who therefore need the hard fist of the Law before they can begin to appreciate the soft, tender hand of the Gospel. And they are also (may I coin an unsatisfactory phrase?) the half-spiritual, whose stew-ardship performance is fairly commendable but whose spiritual life has never gone quite deep enough to be concerned with the thoughts which are troubling you. I say, to them I should have to write quite differently. But right now I am writing to *you*.

Let me begin by saying that the possibility of "stewardship anxiety" is much greater today than it was, say, a hundred years ago. Modern methods of communication have dumped the miseries of the whole world right on our front doorstep. More than that, right into our living rooms. Our forebears knew comparatively little about the crying needs of their fellow men throughout the world; and what they did know was softened by the cushion of time and distance. A weekly newspaper of four pages, with almost no pictures, was in many instances their only window on the world. What happened in China, India, Tibet, or Russia might just as well have happened on Mercury, Venus, Mars, or Jupiter — at least, as far as immediate "stewardship" responsibilities were concerned. A typhoon off the shores of Japan was, for all practical purposes, as far away as a disturbance on the sun. Pestilence, famine, hunger, war, and bloodshed in China, Mongolia, or Siberia were, in effect, "light years" from the plantation owner rocking contentedly on the front porch of his Southern mansion. Either he never heard of them, or, if he did, they were ancient history when they came to his attention — history which had taken place in a land of which he had read only in his school geography. Both the distance and the time lapse removed any "stewardship" claim upon him personally.

How different today! You and I have the whole world between our thumb and forefinger — if we use them to turn on our radio or television set. One flick of the switch, and the agonies of a world estranged from God are spread out before us in our living room — the starving child on the streets of Hong Kong, the corpses in the gutters of Bombay, the homeless refugees in the no man's lands of the Middle East, the squalor of the slums in prosperous U. S. A., the ignorance, the fear, and the superstition in the haunting eyes of the hopeless pagan — these and a hundred other heart-wrenching scenes, for which the devout man is bound to have a feeling of shared responsibility, fairly leap at us from our television screens or reach our ears through our kitchen radio.

And what should we say about the daily newspapers and the weekly magazines? Not to mention church periodicals! These printed media have developed the art of communication to such an extent that the reader can almost say: "I am there!" Color photography, color printing, combined with the consummate skills of the editorial arts have, as it were, taken the reader and transplanted him to the street corners of Calcutta, Bangkok, and Borneo. In a sense he *is* there; for he sees things exactly as they are. And in many cases he sees them or hears about them within hours after they happen — while they can still make a claim upon his stewardship responsibility. I shall not belabor this point any further. Suffice it to say that the tremendous advances in the field of communication, especially during the past fifty years, have contributed materially to what I have chosen to call the "stewardship anxiety" of many devout people.

There is another development in our modern society which is contributing to this stewardship anxiety. I am referring to the methods employed by many religious, educational, and charitable agencies to make their claims upon the stewardship responsibility of the individual. In our day, collecting money — even for the most worthy causes — has become a science. As a rule, only professionals are employed. Elaborate machinery is set up. A battery of clerks is hired. A "system" is soon evolved which, despite the best intentions of those who devised it, becomes completely mechanical and utterly impersonal. The individual donor, both past and prospective, ceases to be an individual human being and becomes merely an address plate or a hole in an IBM punch card. Once his name has been punched into cardboard or embossed on metal, he becomes prospect No. 542,921, and a direct line is established from headquarters to his mailbox. And for months, maybe for years, a steady stream of Macedonian calls will flow through whirling mimeograph machines or rotary presses, shouting, "Come over and help us!" Almost every call is a crisis! And the identical call will go out to No. 542,921 as will go to No. 243,624 because, in the very nature of the case, both are merely numbers in a tray of address plates. To an impersonal machine they simply *cannot* be individual souls with vastly varying sensitivities and infinitely differing spiritual insights. Nor can they be individual human beings with greatly varying financial capabilities.

Now, don't get me wrong! I am not making a blanket indictment of this approach. We are living in a complex and complicated world, and we can thank God for every legitimate device which enables a worthy cause to get its message across to those who are willing and able to support it. In itself there is surely nothing wrong with the use of address plates and IBM cards in the solicitation of offerings for charitable causes. On the other hand, we cannot blink the fact that in some cases, no doubt in many more than some people realize, this mechanical, impersonal, indiscriminate approach to prospective donors has contributed substantially to the stewardship anxiety of which I am writing in this letter.

Recently a distressed young secretary came to me. The sole support of her widowed mother, she was giving a tithe of her modest monthly salary to the congregation in which she was serving as a Sunday school teacher. Referring to a stack of letters which had piled up on her dresser at home, she said: "I don't know what to do any more. I can't turn all those people down, and yet if I send only a dollar or two to each, we'll never be able to meet our bills." Out of the goodness of her heart she had sent modest contributions (as little as a dollar) to more than a dozen worthy causes over a period of two or three years, and in each case she had become an address plate in a highly organized collection machine. Being a sensitive person, wholly dedicated to the cause of Christ, and not aware of the impersonal nature of the collection machinery which had ground out those letters by the thousands, she had considered each urgent appeal as having been directed to her, and to her alone. To her, each letter was a personal request from the president of the college, from the housefather of the orphans' home, from the chaplain of the home for the aged, or from the speaker on the religious radio program, beseeching her, Mary Jones, to come to his rescue. Surely there is no shorter road to stewardship anxiety.

Knowing you as I do, Mark, I wouldn't be a bit surprised if, at least in part, your stewardship anxiety has a similar background. If so, let me tell you what I told this young lady. To begin with, make sure that you are acquainted with the promotional methods, particularly the collection mechanics, which are employed by most charitable organizations today. There is really nothing wrong with the mechanics, provided we are fully acquainted with them. Of necessity, these organizations must make a blanket approach to *all* of their potential donors; they cannot single out each prospective donor and approach him on the basis of his individual capacity to give. In fact, as a rule they do not even *know* their donors personally. The only faces they know are the faces of their address plates.

Since they cannot visit each prospective donor personally, they send out a general mailing to all of the address plates in their trays. If they send out 100,000 letters, they will be very happy to receive financial help from, say, 10,000. They have learned, on the basis of experience, that to receive responses from 10,000 they *must* send letters to 100,000. It may very well be that, because of circumstances best known to you and God, you can with good conscience be one of the 90,000 nonrespondents to a given mailing. It may very well be that of five appeals from a given charity you can respond to only one. If so, thank God that you were able to respond to the one, and do not give yourself over to feelings of guilt because you were unable to respond to the four.

In this connection, learn to discriminate intelligently. It is physically and financially impossible for you to support every worthy undertaking in the world today. You will have to draw a line somewhere. There is nothing unchristian in a courteous post card addressed to a worthy institution asking them to remove your name from their solicitation list. Choose a few worthy charities which are close to your heart and, with God's help, do your best to remember them with offerings according to your ability. Pray for those undertakings which you cannot support financially. In His own way, and in answer to your prayers, the Lord will find donors for those charities to which you are unable to send financial contributions.

This brings me to a still more basic consideration, one which I hesitate to go into, but one which I dare not evade if I want to address myself honestly and frankly to what seems to be your stewardship anxiety. For some time I have been seriously concerned about what seems to be an increasingly emotional approach to the whole question of Christian stewardship. It is an approach which, if consistently pursued, can ultimately lead the spiritually sensitive person to a stewardship neurosis. There can be no doubt about the theology which underlies the Christian doctrine of stewardship. That God is the Maker and Owner of all is abundantly clear from Scripture. "For every beast of the forest is Mine, the cattle on a thousand hills." [1] "The silver is Mine, and the gold is Mine, says the Lord of hosts." [2] Nor can there be any doubt that we ourselves, both body and soul,

[1] Psalm 50:10, 11   [2] Haggai 2:8

are God's possession — that we are His both by right of creation and by right of redemption — and that we are answerable to Him for the use to which we put our entrusted talents: material, mental, and spiritual. Above all, there can be no doubt that we as Christians, motivated by the love of Christ, will want to pray and work and *give* of our material possessions so that the purposes of Christ on earth may be furthered. As Paul puts it, "The love of Christ constraineth us. . . . He died for all, that they which live should not henceforth live unto themselves, but unto Him which died for them and rose again." [3]

I say, Mark, that concerning all of the above there can be no doubt. But having said that, I must also say that there is a way of *applying* the above, particularly in so-called stewardship programs and high-pressure appeals for charity, that is emotional to the point of being fanatic. I have read articles on this subject by well-meaning authors and have heard lectures by well-meaning speakers which, if applied consistently, would make it a sin for any Christian to own an Oldsmobile as long as he could get by with a Chevy, or to own a Chevy as long as he could get by with a Rambler, or to own a Rambler as long as he could get by with a bicycle, or to own a bicycle as long as he could walk. I have heard the doctrine of Christian stewardship presented in ways which, if consistently thought through, would make it a sin to own a diamond ring, a gold wrist watch, a second suit, a second pair of shoes, a Baby Ruth, or an O Henry bar. To follow through consistently on some stewardship presentations, one would have to harbor a sense of guilt concerning one's material possessions until one was reduced to the economic level of a John the Baptist, who "was clothed with camel's hair, and had a leather girdle around his waist, and ate locusts and wild honey," [4] and even then one might feel a little guilty about the honey.

If the above seems a bit facetious, let me assure you it wasn't meant to be. It was meant rather to show you that a purely emotional approach to this whole question can lead to fanaticism. And fanaticism can lead to all sorts of irrationality. It is not a sin to own a home, to own a car, to invest in

[3] 2 Corinthians 5:14a, 15 KJ   [4] Mark 1:6

our children's education, to have a bank account, to enjoy those good things of life which a bountiful God has given His children for their enjoyment; indeed, it is not a sin to be wealthy, if in the administration of our wealth we acknowledge Him as the Giver of all good gifts — including the *intelligence* according to which we administer our affairs to His glory and to the welfare of our fellow man.

The Lord has given each of us some very definite responsibilities very close to home, responsibilities which none of us is free to evade or avoid. The Scriptures tell us that he who fails to provide for his own family "has disowned the faith and is worse than an unbeliever." [5] It is not only sheer fanaticism, it is a form of false religion to press the claims of "stewardship" to the detriment or to the neglect of those basic responsibilities which are ours as members of a Christian family. Caring for our *own* is an essential part of the stewardship which God expects of us. We should never feel that we are robbing God when we use His gifts to take care of the legitimate needs of our loved ones.

I am not saying, Mark, that you and I will ever be completely free from a certain amount of stewardship anxiety. We are dealing here with one of those anxieties which are the inevitable concomitant of the regenerate life — an anxiety, I cannot stress it too often, which is largely unknown to the nonspiritual man or woman. As long as we are both spirit and flesh,[6] as long as we have within us both the promptings of our *old* nature and the promptings of the *new*,[7] we shall be subject to the tensions and the contradictions which are brought about by these opposing voices within us.[8] We are dealing here with one of those distinctively Christian anxieties which can never be completely resolved, except by the death of one of our two natures. We know from Scripture that our old nature, the one which we brought into the world at the moment of birth, is not going to die while we are still on this earth. To be completely freed from spiritual conflicts such as this could, therefore, only mean that our new nature, given us in Christ, had

5 1 Timothy 5:8   6 John 3:1-6
7 Galatians 5:17   8 Romans 7:14-25

died. Thank God that your very anxiety in this respect is the throbbing pulse beat, indicating that your new nature in Christ is still very much alive.

But how are we to *live* in the presence of such contradiction, such unresolved conflict? Do you really think that our heavenly Father expects us to lie awake at night, to tie our wrinkled pillows into knots, to deplete our energies by constantly wrestling with feelings of guilt, and finally to render ourselves unfit for further service to Him and to our fellow man? Surely not!

In the case of stewardship anxiety, as well as all those other peculiarly Christian anxieties which, in their very nature, are unresolvable this side of heaven (evangelism anxiety, for instance), my counsel to you, Mark, is this: always remember that, as a redeemed child of your heavenly Father, you are dealing with a God of infinite grace, not with a celestial Scrooge who is humped over a book in which your eternal doom is sealed. God loves you! In Christ He has done everything that is needed for your eternal happiness. If a particular anxiety is unresolvable (and I am thinking now especially of those anxieties which stem from the inevitable contradictions inherent in the Christian life), do not hesitate to put that particular anxiety into God's hands.[9] Let *Him* live with it. Don't you sleep with it. As the God of infinite compassion He will hold it in His hands while you rest and gather strength for constructive Christian living. If you really have been remiss in your stewardship life, He will have a way of bringing you to sincere repentance. And having brought you to repentance, He will, as He has done a thousand times before, enfold you in His all-embracing love, forgiving you for Jesus' sake. And with His forgiveness in your heart you will go on to higher spiritual levels, also to higher levels of Christian stewardship. If you have been a good steward, as I have every reason to believe that you have, He will have His own way of speaking a "well done" to your heart and encouraging you to continue.

I have said it before, but let me say it once more before I conclude this letter. As I know you, I have every reason to

9 1 Peter 5:7

believe that you have exercised a faithful stewardship over the gifts which God has given you. You have been conscientious in your efforts to support those loved ones whom God has entrusted to your care; and at the same time you have consistently given your generous support to both church and charity. I am sure that God will bless you for this. And I am sure, too, that as the Lord continues to give you the material means, you will continue to use them to His glory.

John

"I get such gloomy thoughts. . . . There are moments when I feel that God has passed me by."

XVIII · In the Hollow of His Hand

Dear Mark:

So God has passed you by!

I am sure that when you see those words in cold print, you will feel uncomfortable for having written them and will be more than willing to retract them. In fact, I am quite sure that you never really *believed* that God has passed you by. You have received too many evidences of His love and of His personal concern for you to believe that seriously. Nevertheless, I think I know what prompted you to write the way you did. There are moments in every person's life when his faith in God's *personal* concern wears thin, when feelings of doubt and insecurity temporarily gain the upper hand, when, at least for the moment, we feel all alone in God's great universe and wonder how He could possibly be concerned about "little us."

The temptation to such thinking is much greater today than ever before in human history. Ours is the age of the sputnik, the man-made satellite, the moon-shot, and the constantly lengthening reach of man into limitless space. The little universe of our forefathers has suddenly opened up into a vast expanse which defies the puny powers of man's imagination. Astronomers, whose mathematics the world has learned to respect, tell us that the sun which gives us light and warmth, and whose size is many times that of our earth, is separated from us by some ninety-three million miles — and that the miles which separate the sun from the planet Neptune have been computed at three hundred million. Dr. Wernher von Braun, noted space scientist and himself a believer, recently said: "Our sun is one of a hundred billion stars in our galaxy, and our galaxy is only one of billions of galaxies populating the universe."

It is only natural that in our weaker moments we ask: Can the God who conceived such an inconceivable vastness, who brought these heavenly bodies into being, and who even today fills every mile between the planets with the power of His presence — can *He* be interested in *me*? Can *He* be interested in *my* fears and worries, my problems and perplexities? *My* life? *My* destiny? And even if He is, can He possibly take time out from His administration of the vast physical universe to do anything about the little hurts, the failures, and the heartaches of one single member of the human family which today numbers some three billion?

The answer, Mark, is, of course He can and He does! A God whose wisdom and omnipotence could create a universe great enough to house the sun, the moon, and the stars will surely be able to house our little lives within the walls of His protecting love. A God who is great enough to do the one is surely great enough to do the other! What you and I must always remember, in the midst of a generation which has come to look upon the entire universe as an impersonal machine, is that *this is our Father's world.* No blind force, no blind fate, no impersonal cosmic necessity, but our Father's love still guides and shapes the destiny of all His children in things both great and small.

Does this sound too sentimental? Too idealistic? Too poetic for the prosaic everyday world in which we live? No doubt, there are times when you and I are tempted to think it is. Then let us remember that it was Christ Himself who assured us of His heavenly Father's concern for *each* of His children. Again and again Christ assured us that God is not only the Father of the human family in general, but that He is the Father of the individual believer in particular — intimately concerned with his everyday needs. "Are not two sparrows sold for a penny? And not one of them will fall to the ground without your Father's will. But even the hairs of your head are all numbered. Fear not, therefore; you are of more value than many sparrows." [1] To Christ there was no contradiction at all between a God who created and sustains the vastness of the universe and a God who is concerned about the minutest needs of the individual. The God who holds the planets in the hollow of His hand also holds the sparrows. "Fear not, therefore; you are of more value than many sparrows."

No, Mark, God has not passed you by. He is right there with you — right where you are today. He is eager that you experience the warmth, the comfort, and the reassurance of His presence. He is eager that you know that His thoughts toward you are thoughts of kindness and of mercy, and that, far from having passed you by, He has securely enfolded you in the arms of His protecting love. To you and to all who have thrown themselves upon His mercy in Christ, He says: "Can a woman forget her sucking child, that she should have no compassion on the son of her womb? Even these may forget, yet I will not forget you. Behold, I have graven you on the palms of My hands." [2]

Perhaps I should say a little more about God's having engraved you on the palms of His hands. Is this merely a figure of speech? Merely a beautiful way of expressing a pious thought which contains more or less truth? No, it is more than that. (In a sense, of course, it *is* a figure of speech, inasmuch as God is a Spirit and has no hands on the palms of which He inscribes the names of those who are His.) In the language of the theologian such expressions as "I have graven you on the palms of My hands" are known as anthropomorphisms — attempts to put into human language *facts* which are true of the Divine. Behind the picture language there is always a divine, eternal, and immutable fact. Behind the language of this passage lies the gilt-edged assurance that you are as close to God and as much

[1] Matthew 10:29, 30   [2] Isaiah 49:15, 16

an object of His daily attention and concern as if your face were inscribed on the palm of His hand. The fact is, in a manner beyond our understanding, *He has inscribed you there!*

What do I mean by that? I mean, as I have said in one of my previous letters, that in ages past, before the world came into being, God decided to choose *you* out of the stream of humankind, to make you the object of His love, to bring you to faith in the Savior, to cleanse you from all sin and guilt, to conform you more and more to the image of His Son, and finally to bring you to Himself to live with Him in all eternity. The point that I am making, Mark, is that God did not choose the human race in general; He chose you in particular. The Bible puts it: "Those whom He foreknew He also predestined to be conformed to the image of His Son, in order that He [Jesus] might be the First-born among many brethren. And those whom He predestined He also called; and those whom He called He also justified; and those whom He justified He also glorified." [3] Addressing one single believer, the apostle Paul writes to his pupil Timothy: "God hath saved us [you and me] and called us with a holy calling, not according to our works, but according to His own purpose and grace, which was given us [you and me] in Christ Jesus before the world began." [4] And listen to the unshakable assurance with which he writes to the Christians at Ephesus: "Even as God chose us in Him [Jesus] before the foundation of the world, that we should be holy and blameless before Him. *He destined us in love to be His sons* through Jesus Christ, according to the purpose of His will, to the praise of His glorious grace which He freely bestowed on us in the Beloved [Jesus]. In Him we have redemption through His blood, the forgiveness of our trespasses, according to the riches of His grace which He lavished upon us." [5]

Now I know, Mark, that some people become frightened as soon as they hear the word "predestined" or "predestination." That does not alter the fact that the Bible does teach a certain type of predestination and that it teaches it very clearly. According to the Bible, any person who has come to faith in

---

[3] Romans 8:29, 30   [4] 2 Timothy 1:9 KJ
[5] Ephesians 1:4-8

Christ as his Savior should be able to say with the apostle Paul: "God has saved *me* and called *me* with a holy calling, not according to my works, but according to His own purpose and grace, which was given *me* in Christ Jesus before the world began." It is extremely significant that whenever the Bible speaks about God's having chosen us in Christ before the foundation of the world, it does so to comfort, to strengthen, to reassure the individual believer. The Bible's doctrine of a divine choice in ages past is never presented as an intellectual proposition to be debated by the spiritually unenlightened; rather, it is always presented, as it were, as a private or a personal message to those who have already come to a saving knowledge of Christ as Lord and Savior.

This is how God wants you to view this entire matter of His having chosen you "in Christ" before the foundation of the world, to be His very own. He wants you, as it were, to take your place at the foot of Calvary, to look up into the face of His divine Son as He hangs there dying for your sin, and then to repeat those words of indescribable comfort and assurance: "God so loved the world that He gave His only-begotten Son, that whosoever believeth in Him should not perish, but have everlasting life." [6] You believe those words, don't you, Mark? I am sure you do. But do you know that you could never believe those words if the Lord, who chose you in ages past to be His own, had not put that faith into your heart? "No man can say, 'Jesus is Lord,' except by the Holy Spirit." [7] Without the enlightening and converting power of God's Holy Spirit you could never lift believing eyes toward the cross of Christ. The very fact that you can, the very fact that you do, is proof that God's Holy Spirit has entered your heart, and His presence there is your guarantee that God has chosen you — yes, *you* — as one of His own. It is with great emphasis and with great significance that the apostle Paul says to the Corinthians: "He who has prepared us for this very thing is God, who has given us the Spirit as a guarantee." [8] Believe me, Mark — or, rather, believe the Scriptures — the very fact that you see in the Christ of the cross your eternal and all-availing Redeemer is your positive

[6] John 3:16   [7] 1 Corinthians 12:3

[8] 2 Corinthians 5:5

guarantee not only of the presence of God's Holy Spirit in your heart but also of your having been engraved in the palms of the Almighty before the foundation of the world.

Does this sound like some farfetched theologizing? Let me quote for you a rather extended portion of one of Paul's epistles. He had just sat down in his prison cell at Rome to write a letter to his Christian converts in the pagan city of Ephesus. Mind you, in Paul's mind he was not undertaking to write a theological treatise. He was writing to friends to confirm them in their new-found faith. After a few words of greeting, here is how he starts his letter:

"Praise be to God for giving us through Christ every possible spiritual benefit as citizens of heaven! For consider what He has done — before the foundation of the world He chose us to become, in Christ, His holy and blameless children, living within His constant care. He planned, in His purpose of love, that we should be adopted as His own children through Jesus Christ — that we might learn to praise that glorious generosity of His which has made us welcome in the everlasting love He bears toward the Son.

"It is through the Son, at the cost of His own blood, that we are redeemed, freely forgiven through that full and generous grace which has overflowed into our lives and opened our eyes to the truth. For God has allowed us to know the secret of His plan, and it is this: He purposes in His sovereign will that all human history shall be consummated in Christ, that everything that exists in heaven or earth shall find its perfection and fulfillment in Him.

"And here is the staggering thing — that in all which will one day belong to Him [Christ] we have been promised a share (since we were long ago destined for this by the One who achieves His purposes by His sovereign will), so that we, as the first to put our confidence in Christ, may bring praise to His glory! And you, too, trusted Him, when you had heard the message of truth, the Gospel of your salvation. And after you gave your confidence to Him, you were, so to speak, stamped with the promised Holy Spirit as a guarantee of purchase [earnest money], until the day when God completes the redemption of what He has paid for as His own." [9]

Let me lift out only a few phrases from this splendid passage to underscore the point which I am trying to make tonight, and to show you that the point is really not mine, but rather that of the Scriptures. "Before the foundation of the world He chose us to become, in Christ, His . . . children." — "He planned . . . that we should be adopted . . . through Jesus Christ." — "For God has allowed us to know the secret of His plan." — "In all which will one day belong to Him [Christ], we have been promised a share." — "We were long ago destined for this." — We are "stamped with the promised Holy Spirit as a guarantee" of our complete and final redemption in glory. In other words, already in eternity past, and also in eternity present, and surely also in eternity future, you and I have been, are, and shall continue to be graven in the palms of our Father's hands. That is the Scripture's assurance.

Now let me repeat that sentence in your recent letter which occasioned my letter to you tonight. You say: "There are moments when I feel that God has passed me by." Admitting that, in our human weakness, all of us experience just such moments, doesn't such a complaint sound utterly groundless on the lips of one who from eternity has been enfolded in the arms of God's redeeming grace? God hasn't passed you by, Mark. He has, in truth, "graven you on the palms of His hands." Through Christ He has made you His. Through His Holy Spirit He has brought you safely into the fold of His redeemed. There isn't a moment of the day or night when all the comforts, all the blessings of the Holy Trinity — Father, Son, and Holy Spirit — aren't there for you to feast your soul upon.

How could the God of heaven ever "pass us by" when, according to His own Word, He is in us and we are in Him — by virtue of our relationship to Him through Christ? Again and again the Scriptures picture all of God's redeemed as being "in Him." [10] St. Paul graphically describes this intimate and inseparable relation in the words: "Your life is hid with Christ

---

[9] Ephesians 1:3-14 P   [10] Colossians 2:6

in God." [11] It is up to us, Mark, with the Spirit's help, to nourish this awareness — to see ourselves more and more, as it were, in the very center of the palm of the Almighty. We must see ourselves there — at the breakfast table; on the way to work; as we go about our daily tasks; as we confront each new problem one by one; as anxieties, fears, and doubts arise; and as we nightly draw the curtain on another day and prepare for sleep. At every hour and in every circumstance, we must see ourselves in the very center of the palm of Him who loves us and who, from all eternity, called us as His own.

Can you really believe that such a God could pass you by? He Himself has given you the answer: "I will not forget you. Behold, I have graven you on the palms of My hands." [12] It was a man who had heard God whispering that assurance to his heart who wrote the immortal words:

> Fear not, I am with thee, oh, be not dismayed;
> For I am thy God and will still give thee aid;
> I'll strengthen thee, help thee, and cause thee to stand
> Upheld by My righteous, omnipotent hand.

> The soul that on Jesus hath leaned for repose
> I will not, I will not, desert to his foes.
> That soul, though all hell should endeavor to shake,
> I'll never, no never, no never, forsake. [13]

No, Mark, God has not passed you by. At this very moment He sees your face, and He reads your name in the very hollow of His hand. You are graven there as the constant object of His love.

John

[11] Colossians 3:3   [12] Isaiah 49:16
[13] Based on Isaiah 41:10

"But how CAN God forgive me, when I go on sinning day after day? I've tried to live as a Christian should, but my record is just one moral failure after another. I don't deserve His mercy. . . ."

XIX · Saints — Because of Him

Dear Mark:

It has always been a source of immeasurable comfort to me — and I am sure it can be a source of comfort to you — that Paul addressed his New Testament letters to people whom he called "saints." If you will look at the opening verses of his various epistles, you will see that he wrote them to the "saints" at Rome, to the "saints" at Corinth, to the "saints" at Ephesus, to the "saints" at Philippi, as well as to the "saints" in other cities of the ancient world. Translated literally, the word which he used for "saints" means "holy ones." So that, if we had been living in his day and had received his letters firsthand, we would actually have read his various salutations as saying: "to the holy people" at Rome or at Corinth or at whatever city we may have lived in.

Now, why do I say that there is comfort in this designation? Simply because the "holy people" to whom Paul wrote were anything but "holy" in the sense in which people use that word today. Among the congregations to whom these letters were addressed there was strife and dissension, envy and petty bickering, backbiting and slander, nasty talk and intemperate language, hypocrisy and dishonesty. Indeed, the catalog of sins which plagued the early Christian congregations was not much different from the catalog of sins which plague the average Christian congregation today. And yet the apostle Paul could address these people as "saints"! Why?

Because, according to the Christian religion, it is possible to be a saint and a sinner at the same time. In fact, not only is it possible; it lies in the very nature of things that, on this side of the grave, every saint *is* a sinner; and every sinner who has put his trust in Jesus Christ, the Savior, is a saint. I know that I have gone into considerable detail in treating this subject in one of my previous letters [Chapter viii], but in view of your subsequent correspondence I believe I should repeat very briefly what I said at that time and then proceed to another aspect of this subject on which I have *not* yet written.

The Bible can speak of the believing sinner as being a saint — as being sinless — because Christ died for him. It is really as simple as that. The blood of Jesus Christ, God's Son, has washed him clean from the guilt and stain of every sin.[1] I need not repeat here all of those crystal-clear Scriptural assurances which tell you that the punishment of our sin was visited upon the sinless Son of God and that, because of His death in our behalf, the tremendous debt which stood against us has been canceled. I am sure you know that, and I am sure you believe it. I am sure, too, you mean it with all your heart whenever you sing:

> Just as I am, without one plea
> But that Thy blood was shed for me
> And that Thou bidd'st me come to Thee,
> O Lamb of God, I come, I come.

What seems to be troubling you is that, having accepted the free salvation which God offers you in Christ, you still see very much in your life that fails to come up to the divine standard. As you put it: "I've tried to live as a Christian should, but my record is just one moral failure after another. I don't deserve God's mercy." In other words, as one who is supposed to be a saint, you are depressed and saddened, perhaps even fright-

---

[1] 1 John 1:7

ened, by your lack of saintliness. You know yourself for what you are — a chronic backslider, a miserable ingrate, a disobedient rebel, a prodigal son — and you find it hard to believe all this talk about your being a saint. "After all, I know what's inside of me! I know myself better than anyone else does! I know I can never lay claim to being morally good — much less to being a saint!"

It is right at this point, Mark, that I should like to share with you a Scriptural insight which should make all the difference in the world. You are a saint in God's sight, not because of what you are, but because of what He, in His mercy, has *declared* you to be. Please read that sentence again. Behind it and beneath it lies a wonderful Scriptural assurance. We may know ourselves to be sinners, utterly undeserving of God's mercy. Be that as it may, He has declared us to be His children, His chosen ones, His saints. His "saints in Christ Jesus." [2]

Did you notice that qualifying phrase? "Saints — in Christ Jesus." We are not saints in ourselves, the Bible tells us. But we are saints "in Christ." Here lies a beautiful new thought. Paul frequently refers to the believer as being "in Christ." I'm sure you remember that comforting and reassuring passage in Paul's letter to the Romans: "There is therefore now no condemnation for those who are in Christ Jesus." [3] Now, what does it mean to be "in Christ"? It means many things, of course. Among other things it means that, having been "baptized into Christ Jesus" [4] we live in Him *spiritually* much as an unborn child lives in the body of his mother *physically*. In Him we find our spiritual sustenance, our spiritual strength, and everything we need to support our spiritual life, such as faith, hope, courage, joy, peace, and the daily vision of ultimate victory with Him in the heavenly kingdom. All of these precious spiritual blessings, the Bible tells us, we have "in Christ."

But being "in Christ" means also something else; and tonight I should like to emphasize this with all the clarity and all the power at my command. It is a precious Bible doctrine that we who believe the Gospel of full and free forgiveness through the blood of Jesus Christ are "in Him" *just as a humble and unworthy*

[2] Philippians 1:1   [3] Romans 8:1   [4] Romans 6:3

peasant in the royal robes of the king. Being in Christ means being in the (borrowed, may I say?) robes of *His* righteousness, *His* holiness. Do you remember the story which Christ told of the great wedding feast? The king opened the doors to the wedding to all who would come, "both bad and good." [5] But according to Oriental custom he provided a special wedding garment for each guest, which was to be worn upon entrance to the banquet hall. No matter how soiled, how torn or tattered, the clothing of the guest, he was welcome at the wedding table in the garments provided by the king. These garments belonged not to the guests but to the royal host. They were placed at the disposal of the guests, "both bad and good," without money and without price. Dressed in these garments, all were alike in the sight of the king.

When Christ told the above story, He was, of course, telling a parable. A parable is an earthly story with a heavenly meaning. And the heavenly meaning of this story is made abundantly clear in other passages of the Bible. St. Paul tells us that the supreme purpose and the greatest glory of his life was to "win Christ and be found *in Him*, not having mine own righteousness, which is of the Law, but that which is through the faith of Christ, the righteousness which is of God by faith." [6] Paul knew very well that he had no righteousness of his own, and yet he was not afraid to stand in the presence of God. And why not? Because He had been convinced by a special revelation of God that he could stand before God's presence "in Christ" — that is, in the righteousness which Christ had won and which God had written to his (Paul's) account. Paul could stand in the presence of God — fully justified, fully accepted — because he was covered with the moral mantle of His Son.

May I suggest, Mark, that on this particular point you make a thorough study of the fourth and fifth chapters of Paul's Letter to the Romans. You may find the language somewhat difficult, even in the RSV and in Phillips' paraphrase, but I am sure that you will get the main drift of these chapters. Namely, that God, through Christ, has provided an *objective* righteousness which exists entirely apart from anything that you or I may do,

[5] Matthew 22:10   [6] Philippians 3:8, 9 KJ

and which He has credited to every member of the human race. The righteousness is *there* — an inexhaustible credit, written to your account and mine. Not because you are you or because I am I, but because God in His immeasurable generosity determined, through His Son, to work out a righteousness which would avail for us all — "both bad and good."

It was not without significance that the prophet Jeremiah, when foretelling the birth of the Savior, said: "And this is the name whereby He will be called: 'The Lord is our Righteousness.'" [7] Christ *is* your Righteousness. You have no righteousness of your own. In this context let me quote once more those reassuring words of Paul to the Corinthians: "God was in Christ, reconciling the world to Himself, not counting their trespasses against them. . . . For our sake He made Him [Christ] to be sin who knew no sin, so that *in Him* we might become *the righteousness of God.*" [8]

I realize that I have become somewhat "theological" on these pages. But the problem which you raise in your letter is nothing else but theological. And you will find your answer to it nowhere else but in the revelation which God has given us in the theology of Scripture. Let me now put it as simply as I can. You ask: "How *CAN* God forgive me, when I go on sinning every day? . . . I don't deserve His mercy." Knowing you as I do, I know that the sins to which you refer are not deliberate acts of willful rebellion against your heavenly Father. If they were, I doubt very much that you would have written me. Your sins are, rather, the symptoms of your human weakness — transgressions over which you grieve because you know that by them you have offended the God of heaven and "justly deserved His punishment." Because of these repeated moral failures you find it difficult to believe that you are really one of God's children, that you are really among His elect. "How can I stand in the presence of God from day to day, presuming upon His grace, asking Him to hear my prayers, speaking to Him as though everything were right between Him and me — when I *know* what a moral mess my life has been?"

Right there, Mark, is where the glorious theology of the

[7] Jeremiah 23:6   [8] 2 Corinthians 5:19-21

previous pages comes in. God doesn't look at your moral mess! He looks at the beautiful robe His loving hands have laid upon you. The robe of the objective righteousness of Christ, which is yours by grace, without money and without price — yours to wear as long as you feel your need of it! God has promised you that, as long as you stand before Him in the wedding garment of His Son, He will not see the soiled and tattered rags of your own unrighteousness; He will see only the snow-white mantle of purity and innocence which Christ has won for you. You may see only the filth and the sordidness which you are bringing Him; He will see only the merits of His divine Son with which He has promised to cover you. In your own heart you may see yourself as the groping, stumbling sinner that you are; but in God's heart you are the redeemed child, whom He has purchased with His blood, and whom He has declared righteous — because of His infinite compassion. Remember, you are still a sinner — weak, erring, failing, stumbling — but in God's eyes you are one of His saints, covered with the garments of holiness purchased by His Son.

When I was a little boy, I learned a prayer which I have prayed almost every night for more than forty years. May I suggest that you make a habit of praying it, too. Not only at bedtime, but throughout the day. I learned it in German, but the English approximates the original in beauty and in meaning:

> Christ Jesus' blood and righteousness
> My beauty are, my glorious dress,
> Wherein before my God I'll stand
> When I shall reach the heavenly land.

Believe me, Mark, we need not wait until we reach the heavenly land in order to stand before God in "Christ Jesus' blood and righteousness." We can come into His presence every minute of the day or night arrayed in that glorious dress. No matter how often or how grievously we have sinned, that garment is still there, ready to cover our guilty lives and to present us holy before the God of our salvation.

No matter what your conscience may tell you, you are a saint, Mark — a saint in Christ. And in Christ you are acceptable to your Father in heaven.

John

"I don't know why, but I'm afraid of getting old. I try my best to shut my mind against the future, but it seems the same old fears come back again and again."

XX · Light at Eventide

Dear Mark:

I suppose that ever since the dawn of history men have had a certain dread of growing old. After they have reached the noonday of life or perhaps have gone part way through its afternoon, they suddenly would like to stop the clock. They have a secret fear of evening. Nor is this at all surprising, when viewed purely from the perspective of unenlightened human reason. To the man for whom night is the end, evening can be only an eerie prelude — a prelude to be avoided at all costs.

This is not to say that the evening hours of life do not have their problems also for the devout believer. Indeed, they do have their very real problems. I need not list these problems for you here. From your letter I gather that you have already listed them in far too great detail, and my repeating them would serve only to underscore them the more heavily. The point that I would like to make this evening is that rather than try to "shut your mind against the future," you should rather *open* it to the promises of God, particularly to those promises which relate specifically to the late afternoon and early evening hours of life.

For God *has* given you some promises for the span of life which lies immediately before you.

I almost hesitate to suggest in this connection that you read the words of the Twenty-third Psalm. This psalm of David is so well known to you that for me to tell you to read it and to ponder it is almost as commonplace as it would be for me to suggest that you eat bread, drink water, or breathe air. But sometimes it pays us to go back to the plain and simple bread of God's Word — those familiar passages which we have long since taken for granted — to find the strength and nourishment our heart and soul so sorely need. At this moment I am thinking of only one verse of that beloved psalm. But to see that verse in its proper context, suppose we read the psalm in its entirety:

> The Lord is my Shepherd, I shall not want.
> He maketh me to lie down in green pastures;
> He leadeth me beside the still waters.
> He restoreth my soul; He leadeth me in the paths of
> righteousness for His name's sake.
> Yea, though I walk through the valley of the shadow
> of death, I will fear no evil; for Thou art with me;
> Thy rod and Thy staff, they comfort me.
> Thou preparest a table before me
> in the presence of mine enemies;
> Thou anointest my head with oil; my cup runneth over.
> Surely, goodness and mercy shall follow me all the days
> of my life and I will dwell in the house of the Lord forever.[1]

Now read that final verse once more. How long does David say the goodness and mercy of the Lord will follow him? Only until tonight? Only until tomorrow? Only as long as David would be king and would occupy the royal palace? Only as long as his money would last? Only as long as he would be in the prime of life, enjoying good health and having the companionship of good friends? No! He says: "Goodness and mercy shall follow me *all the days of my life.*"

That same goodness and mercy which had followed him when he was a shepherd boy on the fields near Bethlehem, which

[1] Psalm 23 KJ

had gone with him when he met the giant Goliath in the open field, which had preserved him when he was persecuted by the infuriated King Saul, which had elevated him to the highest position in the kingdom, which had reclaimed him when he had fallen into the grievous sins of murder and adultery, and which had restored him to loving sonship with the Father — that same "goodness and mercy" would follow him *all the days of his life.* Troubled days there would still be for David. Of this he could be sure. But he could be just as sure that God's goodness and mercy would outlast any troubles which might come his way. When the dust of life's battles would be settled, God's goodness and mercy would still be there!

Surely God's promise to you and to me is just as sure as it was to David. I am referring specifically to His promise to be with us "all the days of our life." God's ability to provide for you and me is not diminished by the passing of the years. His goodness will not be less good tomorrow than it is today. His mercies which have been new to us every morning will not fail. The advancing years may bring with them their multiplied reminders that "swift to its close ebbs out life's little day" — the waning strength, the fading vigor, the slowing step, the blurring vision — but they will also bring with them the multiplied assurances that the Lord is our Shepherd and that, in His safe keeping, we shall not want.

I am reminded of the story which is told of an old retired minister who throughout the eventide of life, until his dying day, received an anonymous note through the mail every second week. Enclosed in each envelope were twenty-five dollars in currency. Evidently the kind act of a grateful parishioner, each note bore the scribbled promise: "More to follow." I need hardly tell you, Mark, that that is God's unbreakable pledge to everyone who puts his trust in His redeeming and protecting love. Every blessing that you and I have received from Him since early childhood has borne the divine imprint: "More to follow." The blessings which we receive today are but the pledge of those which we shall receive tomorrow, and those which we shall receive tomorrow will bear the pledge of heaven: "More to follow." It was such a thought the prophet had in mind when he wrote: "The steadfast love of the Lord *never ceases*. His mercies never come to an end. They are new every morning." [2]

St. John speaks of the inexhaustible goodness and mercy of God, specifically of His Son, our Savior, when he says: "From His fullness have we all received, *grace upon grace*." [3] The picture behind those final three words is something like this: Christ's goodness pours in upon us as the waves of the sea. As soon as the one comes, there is always another close behind, and then another and another. "Grace upon grace." Christ's capacity and willingness to supply our needs, both spiritual and material, are unlimited and eternal.

There is no need in our life, however great or small, that Christ does not know and which He will not fill, if it is necessary for the accomplishment of our life's purpose. (For you and me that purpose is the ultimate enjoyment of God in all eternity.) St. Paul knew something of this limitless reservoir of divine goodness and mercy. That is why he could write to the Christians at Philippi: "My God will supply all that you need from His glorious resources in Christ Jesus." [4] Surely, we who have such a bountiful Savior need never fear that His goodness and mercy may ultimately run out. From His hand we have received, and we shall continue to receive, "grace upon grace." From His limitless spiritual and material supply, as long as heaven and earth shall last, there shall always be "more to follow."

Christ Himself had a comforting word for those whose hearts were filled with worry and anxiety over the prospects of the future. You've heard this particular word repeatedly, but may I suggest that you read it against the background of your admitted fear of approaching old age? Listen to what He says to you:

"I tell you, do not be anxious about your life, what you shall eat, nor about your body, what you shall put on. For life is more than food, and the body more than clothing. Consider the ravens: they neither sow nor reap, they have neither storehouse nor barn, and yet God feeds them. Of how much more value are you than the birds!

2 Lamentations 3:22   3 John 1:16
4 Philippians 4:19 P

"And which of you, by being anxious, can add a cubit to his span of life? If then you are not able to do so small a thing as that, why are you anxious about the rest? Consider the lilies, how they grow; they neither toil nor spin; yet I tell you, even Solomon in all his glory was not arrayed like one of these. But if God so clothes the grass which is alive in the field today and tomorrow is thrown into the oven, how much more will He clothe you, O men of little faith? And do not seek what you are to eat and what you are to drink, nor be of anxious mind. For all the nations of the world seek these things; and your Father knows that you need them. Instead, seek His kingdom, and these things shall be yours as well." [5]

Let me pick out only one sentence from this well-known statement of the Savior for your special comfort and encouragement. "Your Father knows." Do not give way to faithless worry, the Savior tells us, because *"your Father knows"* your inmost thoughts and your deepest needs. The weary child at the close of day will often confide his wants and needs to his earthly father and then drift off to peaceful slumber. It is enough that father knows! His love will find a way. His love will contrive the means to satisfy tomorrow's needs. It is enough – if father knows! If that is true of an earthly father, how much more true must it be of our heavenly Father! Not only does our heavenly Father know our every want and wish, but, being the omnipotent God of heaven, He is abundantly able to provide. "He who did not spare His own Son but gave Him up for us all, will He not also give us all things with Him?" [6] The Father who out of infinite love sent His only-begotten Son into this world to be your Savior and mine, would He let us down, would He cheat us, would He mock us by withholding from us anything that is necessary for our eternal bliss and glory?

Afraid of tomorrow? Afraid of the future? Afraid of the lengthening shadows which presage the eventide of life? Why should we be? Our heavenly Father has already lived through all of our tomorrows. He not only knows what tomorrow holds – He holds tomorrow! And to those who have come to Him through Jesus Christ, the Savior, He has promised that there is

[5] Luke 12:22-31   [6] Romans 8:32

nothing in any of our tomorrows that can pluck us from His hands.[7] It is a beautiful and faith-strengthening thought, Mark, this thought of our God in heaven holding all of our tomorrows. It reminds me of an illustration I heard many years ago. A traveler in the Scottish highlands once saw a cluster of colorful flowers far down the mountainside. He promised a reward to a shepherd boy if he would "climb down" the side of the mountain and pick them, offering to let him down by a rope. The boy eyed the stranger suspiciously and then, without a word, disappeared into the woods. In a moment he was back, but with him was his father. He was perfectly willing to be let down the mountainside, *provided the rope was in his father's hands!*

For you and me, Mark, the rope is *always* in our Father's hands! What a reassuring thought! Sometimes our Father in heaven permits our feet to come upon steep and slippery places, down the mountainside of human trial and trouble; but no matter how deep the valley or how difficult the descent, we can always rest secure in the conviction that our times are in His hands. He holds the rope! We shall go just so far down the hillside as His love would have us go. He knows our strength, and He knows our weakness. He knows already before we go down into the valley what flowers we are to bring back with us — what lesson in trust, what lesson in humility, what lesson in Christian virtue — and He will bring us up again as soon as we have gathered the flowers for which His love has sent us.

If ever there was a man who knew what it meant to descend from the mountaintop of prosperity and good fortune down into the abyss of bitter disappointment, that man was David, the man after God's own heart. Small wonder that David on one occasion, when he felt the ground crumbling from beneath his feet and saw the tortuous road below, cast a pleading eye heavenward and exclaimed: "My times are in Thy hand." [8] David knew that, through faith in God's unchanging promises, he had placed his hand into the hand of God, and that God would never let him go. You can have the same assurance that David had. If the Lord in His wisdom should allot you another ten or twenty or thirty years of life, your times will always be in His hands.

[7] John 10:28, 29   [8] Psalm 31:15

No matter what the circumstance, it will be He who holds the rope that keeps your feet from danger.

Do you remember the lines:

> I am trusting Thee, Lord Jesus;
> Never let me fall.
> I am trusting Thee forever
> And for all.

By your Baptism, by your public profession of faith in Him as Lord and Savior, by your frequent partaking of the Sacrament of His body and blood, by your constant worship and ceaseless prayers, you have put yourself into His care and keeping. Do you suppose that He would ever let you fall? His word to you is still the word of the Old Testament promise: "Fear not, for I am with you. Be not dismayed, for I am your God. I will strengthen you. I will help you. I will uphold you with My victorious right hand." [9] To you, to me, and to every believer who has passed the noonday of life He says: "Even to your old age I am He, and to gray hairs I will carry you. I have made [you], and I will bear [you]; I will carry and will save [you]." [10] The eternal God has pledged undying faithfulness to you through every changing scene — through infancy, childhood, youth, manhood, and old age.

It would be wrong, however, Mark, to look upon the evening hours of life as something to be "borne" — as an unpleasant prospect for the endurance of which we shall need a special measure of God's grace. It is true, we need His grace for every period of our life, but there is no reason to believe that old age will call for a special measure. "I need Thy presence every passing hour" can be sung with just as much truth by the robust teen-ager as by the gray-haired grandfather. Far from looking upon old age as a time of gathering shadows, we can regard it as a time of gathering brightness. As the prophet Zechariah says in a different context: "At evening time there shall be light." [11] Indeed, in the Christian life there is a light at eventide toward which the believing heart may well look forward — not in fear, but in hope and eager expectation. It is the light which

[9] Isaiah 41:10   [10] Isaiah 46:4   [11] Zechariah 14:7

comes with spiritual maturity, the light which bathes the mountain peak while all the valleys lie in shadow, the light which enabled the old man Simeon, after a life of patient waiting, to exclaim: "Mine eyes have seen!" [12]

Toward the end of the Book of Job there is a passage which, I fear, all too often escapes the attention of the casual reader. The book is almost over, and we hear Job addressing God. He says: "I had heard of Thee by the hearing of the ear, but now my eye sees Thee." [13] In his younger years Job had indeed heard and spoken much about God, for he was a pious man. But, as he now admits, much of what he had known about God was merely by "the hearing of the ear." As the years progressed and his spiritual insight deepened, he learned to know God in an altogether different way. "Now my eye *sees* Thee!" Now that he was in the upper grades in the school of life, he no longer had to be content with a hearsay knowledge of God; now he saw Him! The Spirit of God had used the crushing experiences of Job's life to open his eyes to the love and the faithfulness of God his Savior. And so for Job, as for everyone who puts his trust in the redeeming love of God, the evening hours of life were much brighter than its noonday. Whereas in the prime of life he had only "heard," in the dusk of life he "saw." He saw his God!

For the believer in Christ, life is a constant and progressive revelation of the love and faithfulness of God. The longer he lives, the more convinced he becomes both of his own unworthiness in the presence of his Maker and of the all-sufficiency of God's abounding grace. Many a seemingly commonplace Scriptural assurance which in his childhood he has indeed learned "by the hearing of the ear" has taken on added meaning and has given him deeper solace as he passed from life's noonday into its eventide. Such assurances of the Savior as "God so loved the world . . .";[14] "Come unto Me, all ye that labor and are heavy laden . . .";[15] "Let not your heart be troubled . . .";[16] and "Lo, I am with you always . . ." [17] which in his youth were nothing more than "Bible passages," have become veritable powerhouses of spiritual strength. The passing years have taught him the

[12] Luke 2:30	[13] Job 42:5	[14] John 3:16
[15] Matthew 11:28	[16] John 14:1	[17] Matthew 28:20

beauty and the sweetness and the unfailing trustworthiness of these divine assurances. What he has heard in his youth he has seen in his old age. He has seen the love of God at work in human hearts. He has seen it sufficient to meet all needs. Above all, he has seen it sustain him in every changing scene of life, and he is willing to continue to lean upon that love all the way.

Have I been sounding too theological again tonight? Too theological to be practical? Had you hoped that I would devote this letter more specifically to the social and economic problems which frequently attend old age in our complex society? I fully agree that these problems are real and that you will ultimately have to address yourself to them — as they present themselves in due course. Nevertheless, your *first,* and by far your most important, step toward banishing your fears of the future, especially your fears of old age, *must* be theological. At the root of all our deepest fears is our relationship to God — or the lack of such relationship. Once we have let Him put our hand in His, we shall not have to worry about any part of the road which lies before us, be it the bend which lies just ahead or the unseen stretch which lies closest to our journey's end.

If we know, with the assurance that only His Holy Spirit can give us, that we are His today (and from your frequent assertions of faith in Christ as Lord and Savior I am sure that you are numbered as His own), then we can also be sure that we will still be His tomorrow. And if we are His, what permanent evil can befall us? St. Paul was an old man when he wrote his second letter to the young pastor Timothy. Listen to the confidence with which he wrote, even though he was writing in a Roman prison, fully aware that he would soon meet a martyr's death:

"For I know the One in whom I have placed my confidence, and I am perfectly certain that the work He has committed to me is safe in His hands until that Day. . . . I feel that the last drops of my life are being poured out for God. The glorious fight that God gave me I have fought; the course that I was set I have finished, and I have kept the faith. The future for me holds the crown of righteousness which God, the true Judge, will give to me in that Day — and not, of course, only to me but to all those who have loved what they have seen of Him." [18] Do you see how clearly Paul's theology was the basis for the almost careless and defiant courage with which he faced old age? Paul knew not only *about* the One in whom He had put his confidence, He *knew the One*. And He was "perfectly certain" that that One would take care of him until the day appointed.

You know the same One, Mark. You know Him just as well and just as effectively as did the apostle Paul. Right now the clouds of doubt may have obscured your vision of Him just a little, but He is still there, and His omnipotent hand is still holding yours in His. He is the God of your childhood, the God of your youth, and He will be the God of your old age. You have staked your life, your whole eternity on Jesus Christ, who is "the same yesterday and today and forever." [19] He will be the same Savior, mighty to comfort and mighty to uphold, when you are old as He was when you were young.

No, Mark, do not try to shut your mind against the future. Open it! Open it to the soul-sustaining promises of Him who loves you and who has promised to be with you — all the way.

John

[18] 2 Timothy 1:12; 4:6-8 P
[19] Hebrews 13:8

*"If only I could control the thoughts that come into my mind!
Many of them are so distressingly negative and result only in
discouragement and depression. Some of them are downright
unworthy and make me so ashamed."*

XXI · Thoughts That Lift

Dear Mark:

This evening I shall try to reply to a number of questions
which you have posed in your recent correspondence. First,
a few words about those "distressingly negative thoughts" which
seem to be causing you serious concern. I suppose, if the truth
were told, negative thinking is a malady which afflicts most of
us to a greater or lesser degree. In saying that, I do not wish
to condone or to justify the habit of negative thinking; nor
do I wish to minimize the debilitating (sometimes even paralyzing) effects it has on those who succumb to it. In fact, one
need not be a professional psychiatrist to point out that negative
thinking, if indulged in consistently, can be a dangerous form
of self-hypnosis.

Hypnosis, as you know, is nothing more than the power
of intense and repeated suggestion. The hypnotist achieves his
purpose by riveting the conscious mind of his subject on some
extraneous or irrelevant object and then slipping past the
conscious mind to the subconscious with the type of thoughts

he wishes to implant. I'm sure you've seen a hypnotist put his subject to sleep by saying: "You are very, very tired. Very, very sleepy. Very, very drowsy. You are completely relaxed. Your arms are limp. Your hands are heavy. You are losing all sensation. You are very, very tired. Very, very sleepy. Very, very drowsy. Now you are — asleep." Now, why did the subject fall asleep? Simply because his subconscious mind reacted to the positive suggestions regarding sleep. In the final analysis, that was all there was to it. By the same token, we can exert a tremendous influence on our day-to-day attitudes, our behavior, our personality, yes, even our character, by the type of thoughts we continue to feed both to our conscious and to our subconscious mind.

This, of course, is really nothing new. Solomon in the Book of Proverbs tells us: "As he [that is, any person] thinketh in his heart, so *is* he." [1] Recently we read an article entitled: "You Are What You Eat." No doubt there is more than a little truth to that intriguing title. There would be even more truth to an article entitled: "You Are What You Think." In our most honest moments, in those moments when we stand alone in the presence of our God, we shall have to admit that, in the final analysis, we are not what we say, not what we do, not what we look — but we are ultimately what we *think*. Or to put it another way, it is the thoughts we think that determine what we are, and not the words we say, the deeds we do, or the changing expression of our facial features. David, the man whose mind had conceived dark thoughts of which he was thoroughly ashamed, knew this very well. That is why he prayed that not only "the words of my mouth" but also and especially "the meditation of my heart" might be acceptable "in Thy sight, O Lord, my Rock and my Redeemer." [2]

I believe, Mark, that in controlling those thoughts which you describe as "so distressingly negative" and so "downright unworthy," you will do well to start where David did. With God. I know that to some this advice may seem highly impractical, perhaps even a little fatuous. But you and I dare never forget that it is God who is the Source, the Fountainhead

[1] Proverbs 23:7 KJ   [2] Psalm 19:14

of all that is good and clean and true and noble. In the Letter of James we are told that: "Every good endowment that we possess . . . must come from above, from the Father of all lights." [3] Paul told the Philippian Christians: "It is God who is at work within you, giving you the will and the power to achieve His purpose." [4] It is to God, the Source of all light and all purity, to whom we shall have to turn in the first instance, if we are to exchange those "distressingly negative" and "downright unworthy" thoughts for thoughts which will meet with His approval.

I shall not elaborate here on what I mean by turning to God. As a believer in Christ, you know what I mean. But let me put it briefly. Draw constantly closer to your Lord by an ever more consistent use of His Word and Sacrament. Cultivate, even more assiduously than before, the practice of personal devotions. Make a habit of joining with your fellow believers as they gather around the Word of God Sunday after Sunday — both in Bible class and in formal worship. Take part, as frequently as you possibly can, in the celebration of the Lord's Supper, which will prove not only a spiritual cleansing for your heart and soul but also a spiritual tonic, giving you the inner strength to carry on the daily battle against the forces which are trying to pull you downward. Direct your mind daily, hourly, to the great thoughts of God's revelation which He has given you in the Sacred Scriptures: thoughts of Christ, His death for you on Calvary's cross, His resurrection, His ascension, His sitting at the right hand of God in glory, His rule of grace over the whole family of His redeemed, His imminent return to take you and me from this vale of tears to Himself to live forever in the mansions of His Father.

After the great miracle on the Mount of Transfiguration, we are told of Peter, James, and John that "when they lifted up their eyes, they saw no one but Jesus only." [5] I submit, Mark, that one of the first steps in dealing with negative and unworthy thoughts is to cultivate the habit of lifting our eyes away from ourselves and away from the horizontal perspective of life — and

[3] James 1:17 P   [4] Philippians 2:13 P
[5] Matthew 17:8

seeing "no one but Jesus only." The story is told of a mother who visited her boy at college. Upon entering his room, her eyes swept across the walls, which were covered with more than a dozen suggestive pictures. Her heart was grieved, but she decided to say nothing for the moment. Several days later the mailman delivered a package to the young man. It was a gift from his mother, a beautifully framed picture of the head of Christ. Proudly the boy hung the picture on the wall above his desk. That night, before he went to bed, he removed the pin-up picture which hung closest to the face of Christ. The next day another picture was consigned to the wastebasket. Day after day the pictures began to disappear from the walls until only one remained — the picture of the Savior. No one had lectured to the boy, no one had told him to remove the other pictures. The power of the contemplation of Christ had made it impossible for him to keep the other pictures on the wall. The same thing can happen to the walls of our heart — to the walls of our mind. As Christ is given the pre-eminence in our daily thoughts, the dirty pictures will begin to disappear.

Perhaps you wonder why I did not begin this evening by exhorting you to prayer. I intentionally did not begin by pointing you to prayer, not because I do not consider prayer of great importance in this connection, but rather because I first wanted to emphasize the supreme necessity of the contemplation of Christ as the object of all our thoughts and aspirations. It is Christ who can give us noble thoughts; not only the Christ who dwells within us but also (and this is what I wanted to emphasize especially tonight) the Christ who dwells *above* us. The objective Christ, the Christ of history, the Christ who walked the dusty roads of Palestine and who today rules all things in earth and heaven [6] — this objective, historical Christ must more and more become the object of all our meditation. Some people have a way of making prayer a very subjective thing, as though by their repeated and agonized petitions they themselves were going to produce the thing for which they ask. Although they may not be aware of it, such people have put their faith in prayer — and not in Christ. And believe me, Mark, in the context in

[6] Colossians 1:15-20

which I am writing this evening, such praying can easily end up in quicksand. Simply to sit idle or to wring our hands and whine to the Lord about the negative and unworthy thoughts which plague us can itself become a very negative exercise. I am afraid that many a prayer has not only been a model of negative thinking itself but has also pushed the pray-er down deeper into the morass from which he was seeking to escape. For the negative thinker to lose himself in his own thoughts while he is praying is (or at least *can* be) to lose himself in negative thinking. If he must lose himself, let him lose himself in Christ. It is in Christ that the solution of his problem must be found.

Having said that, let me be quick to assert that prayer does have a place in the therapy of negative thinking. I like the simple directness as well as the positive tone of the prayer of David: "Let the words of my mouth and the meditation of my heart be acceptable in Thy sight, O Lord, my Rock and my Redeemer." [7] There is no reason why you and I should not approach the Lord daily with a prayer that He guide all our thoughts and words and deeds. In fact, every time we pray the Lord's Prayer we are doing just that. But having prayed, trusting in His promise, let us go about our daily tasks in a cheerful mood doing our very best, with His help, to make our prayers come true.

Don't ever think that the answer to such a prayer is not going to call for some doing on our part! As I have pointed out previously, the Christian life of sanctification — and that includes the daily battle with negative and unworthy thinking — is a life-long struggle. With God's help we can make progress as we grow to spiritual maturity. But it is going to call for daily, conscious effort on our part. I am reminded of a statement that is attributed to Martin Luther. Speaking of the sinful thoughts which frequently plague the believer, he is supposed to have said: "We can't stop the birds from flying over our heads, but we can surely keep them from making nests in our hair." As long as you and I live in a world which is charged with wicked thinking, we shall not be able to escape the occasional, perhaps

[7] Psalm 19:14

even repeated, incursion of wicked thoughts into our mind. But surely, with God's help, we can keep those thoughts from taking up permanent residence there.

Let me caution against a futile approach to this whole problem to which, I fear, many have succumbed. There is much more to this whole business than merely getting rid of negative or unworthy thoughts. In fact, the concept of "getting rid" is itself a sign of negative thinking. We shall succeed in this whole matter, not in the measure in which we empty our minds of sinful and degrading thoughts, but rather in the measure in which we *fill* them with thoughts that are wholesome and uplifting. The human mind can never be a vacuum. He who thinks he can improve the tenants of his soul simply by evicting those that are unworthy will find that for every unworthy tenant he evicts through the back door several more will enter through the front.[8] It is not merely a matter of evicting. It is also a matter of screening, selecting, admitting, and cultivating those tenants that have proved themselves desirable. Applying this analogy to your present problem, it is not merely a matter of getting rid of the ugly thoughts which make our lives so miserable, it is also a matter of consciously reaching out for the good and noble thoughts, cultivating first their acquaintance and then their friendship, and finally making them feel at home with us.

I am reminded here of a striking passage in one of Paul's epistles. He is bringing his letter to the Philippians to a close, and as a sort of parting exhortation and encouragement he writes: "Rejoice in the Lord always; again I will say, Rejoice. . . . Have no anxiety about anything, but in everything by prayer and supplication with thanksgiving let your requests be made known to God. And the peace of God, which passes all understanding, will keep (guard) your hearts and your minds in Christ Jesus. Finally, brethren, *whatever is true,* whatever is honorable, whatever is just, whatever is pure, whatever is lovely, whatever is gracious, if there is any excellence, if there is anything worthy of praise, think about these things . . . and the God of peace will be with you."* [9]

8 Matthew 12:43-45
* Ethically true. Therefore morally upright.
9 Philippians 4:4-9

Here was Paul's first-century prescription for spiritual and mental hygiene. What he is saying in effect is this: Keep your mind fixed at all times on the God of your salvation, the God who has chosen you in Christ, the God who has forgiven you all your sins and has adopted you into the glorious family of His redeemed. Let all your gladness be rooted in Him, for He is the only Source of light and joy. And since through Christ you have learned to know Him as your loving, forgiving, and provident Father, don't have a worry in the world. Don't let your mind be clouded by anxious thoughts. But when such thoughts *do* come, go right to God! Just lay your thoughts before Him — open, as it were, upon the table. He will know what to do with the thoughts that trouble you. But as for you [I am still paraphrasing the above passage from Paul], as for you, you just go on thanking Him for all the wonderful things He has done for you. And as you lose yourself in thoughts of gratitude, you will find His peace filling your heart — yes, not only filling it but also keeping it and guarding it against all the assaults of your spiritual enemies. And with His divine peace standing guard over your heart, you will find it possible more and more to devote your thoughts to things that are morally beyond reproach, to things that are respectable, honest, pure, well pleasing to God, and well thought of by men. — If Paul had been writing in the twentieth century, that is, essentially at least, how he would have worded his celebrated words of encouragement to the Philippians.

Before leaving this wonderfully reassuring passage of Paul, let me pick out one significant phrase for special emphasis. "Have no anxiety about anything," he says, "but . . . with *thanksgiving* let your requests be made known to God." I know of few more effective antidotes for spiritual anxiety in general and for negative and "unworthy" thinking in particular than the Christian grace of gratitude. The truly thankful heart, that is, the heart that is truly grateful to God for the marvelous salvation He has provided through His Son, as well as for His daily guidance, protection, and provision, has little room for negative and unworthy thinking. Gratitude is fertile soil for praise, barren soil for grumbling or complaint. Or does this, again, sound too theological or too theoretical? Then let me suggest, Mark, that you try putting it into practice the next time you see yourself losing the battle with your negative thoughts. Instead of (mentally) wringing your hands and whimpering to God for help, just start *thanking* Him, sincerely and fervently, for all the immeasurable blessings He has given you. Not blessings in general, but blessings in particular. Start naming them and listing them. You will be surprised how a prayer of gratitude, fervently and sincerely uttered, can put a host of negative thoughts to flight.

In the measure in which you will ventilate your mind with the bracing and refreshing air of gratitude to God, in that measure you will make it impossible for the dark and corroding thoughts of envy, resentment, and hostility to gain control of your thinking. You don't mention in your letter just what these "unworthy" thoughts are that have been troubling you. Whatever they are, let me suggest that you face up to them frankly and trace them to their source. More often than most people are willing to admit, much of their negative thinking is traceable to an unexpressed hostility toward the world in general, a hostility which frequently has its roots in smoldering resentment or hurt pride. It is so easy for us to sulk, to brood, to glower at the world, to carry a mental chip on our shoulder until we are thoroughly convinced that the whole human race is against us. I submit, Mark, that even thoughts of hostility and resentment will finally yield to the therapy of gratitude. The heart that is truly grateful, consciously and articulately grateful to God for all His mercies, will not prove a congenial place for envy and resentment. For gratitude is the twin sister of humility, and humility knows no "hurt pride," envy, or resentment.

But there is another approach to this business of negative thinking that I would like to suggest, and that is the approach of positive *action*. A friend of mine is the chaplain at a state institution. During one of his pastoral visits a depressed woman came up to him and complained about her "nervousness" and about her melancholy mood. The chaplain, a veteran of nearly fifty years in institutional work, pointed to a long row of women in the ward and suggested that the complaining person work out a program of help for each of her ward mates — writing letters for those who couldn't write, running errands for those confined to wheel chairs, reading the evening paper to those whose sight was failing, engaging in friendly conversation with those who never had visitors. A few weeks later he met the same woman and inquired how she was feeling. "Oh, fine," she replied, and then she began enumerating the things she had done that day. Somehow she had no time to tell him of her "nervousness" or of the melancholy thoughts that had plagued her. The fact of the matter was that she had *forgotten* about her "nervousness" because her mind had been directed to a program of constructive action.

May I suggest a similar approach to you? I don't mean that you are not now an active person. Indeed, I know that you are. But sometimes even active people fall into the habit of setting aside what I might call "devotional periods" during the course of each day, during which they devote themselves exclusively to the nurture of negative thoughts. These periods become a sort of "oasis" to which they look forward for the "enjoyment" of the luxury of self-pity or for a rehashing of old resentments.

I met a man once who said: "I can take care of my thoughts from Monday through Friday, but, oh, how I dread Saturday and Sunday!" The necessity of earning a living by hard work had imposed upon him a program of activity which kept him too busy for "unworthy" thinking during the day and too tired even to *think* when the day was over. But he had no such program for Saturdays and Sundays, and it was on those days that his negative thoughts ran wild. You yourself will know best whether or not there are gaps in your daily or weekly schedule, gaps of unproductive idleness, which provide field days for negative thinking on your part. If there are, make a deliberate and determined effort to fill those gaps as soon as possible. Fill them with constructive and purposeful activity, preferably activity in behalf of others; for there is no better way of *getting your thoughts off your thoughts* than by getting constructively involved in service to your fellow man.

One more point before I bring this letter to a close. There is a bit of advice in Paul's Letter to the Galatians which has a definite bearing on this whole matter of negative and unworthy thinking. "Live your whole life in the Spirit," he says, "and you will not satisfy the desires of your lower nature." [10] I need not point out to you that the word "Spirit" is here spelled with a capital "S" and that the reference, therefore, is to the Third Person of the Holy Trinity — the *sanctifying* Spirit of God. The Bible urges the believer to live his whole life in the Spirit, much as a physician will occasionally urge a patient to live his whole life in a certain climate. Just as a physical illness which could prove fatal in one climate will gradually yield to the healthful air of another, so the corroding and corrupting forces of the flesh will gradually yield to the sanctifying power which comes with "living in the Spirit." The important thing is that we actually *live* our lives in the Spirit, that we center our inmost thoughts and aspirations on *God* and on the promptings of His Holy Spirit. He will give us thoughts that lift.

May I suggest, Mark, that you pray daily for an increasing measure of God's Holy Spirit and that you yield yourself ever more fully to His gracious guidance. There is a beautiful promise in the Gospel according to St. Luke. Jesus tells us: "If you then, who are evil, know how to give good gifts to your children, how much more will the heavenly Father give the Holy Spirit to those who ask Him?" [11] Ask Him, Mark! And continue to ask! As His Holy Spirit takes over your life more and more, you will find the words of your mouth and the meditation of your heart becoming more and more acceptable in the sight of Him who is your Rock and your Redeemer.

John

[10] Galatians 5:16 P   [11] Luke 11:13

"I am frustrated to the point of despair. If the apostle Paul and other believers could 'do all things through Christ, who strengthened them,' why is it that so many of the things that I have undertaken in the name of Christ have ended up in failure?"

XXII · The Christ Who Strengthens

Dear Mark:

This evening I shall do my very best to clear up one difficulty mentioned in your recent letter. You say that you are frustrated to the point of despair, because, far from being able to accomplish "all things through Christ," you have accomplished very little in His name. In a way I am happy that, at least by inference, you are attributing your disappointment and frustration to the failure of a specific Bible statement to come true in your own experience. The Bible statement to which you allude is Paul's assertion: "I can do all things through Christ, which strengtheneth me." [1] I am glad that you have measured your personal failures by this specific passage, because it gives me the opportunity to put this passage into its proper frame of reference for you.

Few misapplications of Scripture have led to more spiritual anxiety than the misapplication of these frequently quoted words of Paul. More than once I have heard them spoken from the

[1] Philippians 4:13 KJ

pulpit in a way which could produce nothing but disillusionment, frustration, and spiritual anxiety. It is utter folly to take these words out of their context and to apply them in such a way as to guarantee complete and unconditional "success" to every project undertaken by the believer in Christ. I have no warrant to assume that by invoking these words of the apostle I can walk down to the banks of the Mississippi tomorrow morning and command its waters to reverse their course. I cannot, by appealing to these words, stand in front of an oncoming loco-motive and command it to stop. Surely, the assertion "I can do all things" must be understood in its proper context and in the light of its intended meaning.

What was that context? May I suggest that you read it in Philippians 4:10-13. Paraphrased, these verses would read some-what as follows: "Please, don't worry about me, my dear Philip-pians. I've learned in the school of experience to be content in whatever circumstances I might find myself. I've learned how to get along in the midst of poverty, I've learned how to get along in the midst of plenty. In fact, I've become quite an authority on what it means to be hungry and on what it means to be full, for I have both endured hunger and I have enjoyed plenty. And do you know what my secret has been — for both *enduring* and enjoying?" In this context he now pro-ceeds to say: "My secret is simply this: I can do all things through Christ, which strengtheneth me." It was Christ who had enabled him both to *endure* and to *enjoy:* to endure not only hunger and poverty but also disappointment, disillusionment, persecution, stoning, and scourging; to enjoy not only food and plenty but also the peace and the joy which were his in the Gospel and the many spiritual victories which God in His grace had given him.

The point which I am trying to make is that one of the things which Christ had enabled Paul to do was to suffer, to endure, successfully. Not only is this clear from the immediate context, but it is also clear from the entire story of Paul's life. Don't forget that the man who boasted that he could "do all things through Christ" carried a bodily affliction with him throughout his adult years — carried it, indeed, all the way to his grave. He was unable, by a wave of the magic wand of faith, to rid himself of his thorn in the flesh. The thing that Christ enabled him to do was to live with this thorn successfully and to use it to Christ's greater glory.[2] Don't forget, too, that the man who could "do all things through Christ" was the man who was *NOT* able to avoid the hardship and the persecution, the anguish and the anxiety, which went with the preaching of the Gospel. Do you remember the credentials of apostleship which he offered to the Corinthians? "Five times I have received at the hands of the Jews the forty lashes less one. Three times I have been beaten with rods; once I was stoned. Three times I have been shipwrecked; a night and a day I have been adrift at sea; on frequent journeys, in danger from rivers, danger from robbers, danger from my own people, danger from Gentiles, danger in the city, danger in the wilderness, danger at sea, danger from false brethren; in toil and hardship, through many a sleepless night, in hunger and thirst, often without food, in cold and exposure. And, apart from other things, there is the daily pressure upon me of my anxiety for all the churches. Who is weak, and I am not weak? . . . If I must boast, I will boast of the things that show my weakness." [3] The man who spelled out this catalog of personal misery is the same man who asserted: "I can do all things through Christ, which strengtheneth me." Stepping back from these words for a moment and seeing them in their total setting, it is not difficult to arrive at their intended meaning. Paul was simply saying that he was prepared to cope with any situation that life might hurl at him, because he had the power of Christ sustaining him.

I am sure you can see, Mark, what a misconstruction of these words it is to use them as a guarantee of "success" as that word is ordinarily used today. Who would be so heartless as to assure the aspiring young singer with no more than an ordinary voice that she can ultimately become an opera star because she can do all things through Christ, who strengthens her? Who would be foolish enough to tell the tone-deaf youngster struggling with his first violin that someday he can become a second Fritz Kreisler simply because he can do all things through Christ, who strengthens him? Indeed, and this comes

---

[2] 2 Corinthians 12:7-10   [3] 2 Corinthians 11:24-30

much closer to home, who would presume to tell the young minister about to enter his first parish that his will be a long and illustrious ministry, that his sermons will be eloquent, his parish administration efficient, his building programs successful — because he can do all things through Christ, who strengthens him? What if two years later he suffers a nervous breakdown and must leave the ministry? Has something gone wrong with the divine promise? Not at all! There was no such divine promise in the first place. The promise was that Christ would sustain him, *no matter what!* Even in the midst of what at the moment may seem like abject failure the power of Christ would be there to sustain him and to see him through.

I am reminded here of an almost frantic letter which I received from a young lady about a year ago. A devout Christian, she had set her heart on becoming a competent, top-notch secretary. But after having been "let out" of two or three secretarial positions because of unsatisfactory work, she was on the verge of despair. In her moment of desperation she quoted these very words of Paul ("I can do all things") and wanted to know why they had not worked for her. She had prayed and prayed to Christ for help, but His help had not been forthcoming. I had to remind her that nowhere has God promised that every believer in Christ will make an efficient secretary. Indeed, some believers in Christ make far better mothers and housewives than secretaries. And I had to remind her that *one* of the "all things" that Christ enables His followers to do is to accept disappointment graciously and victoriously — as, indeed, this passage in its total context so clearly indicates. If experience proved that she was not cut out to be a secretary, the sustaining power of Christ would enable her to take this disappointment in stride and would enable her to be content and to find an equally satisfying sense of purpose in some other kind of work. At the very moment of "failure" she would experience more clearly than ever before the sustaining power of Christ picking her up and carrying her forward to whatever new experience a gracious God in heaven had in store for her.

This young lady, as many others, had made a mistake against which I should like to speak a word of caution. There is a real danger in the glib and thoughtless repetition of religious slogans which are frequently only half- or quarter-truths or which, at best, are only shallow misapplications of profound religious principles. (The motto which I've seen on many desks is a good example. The motto reads "Prayer Changes Things." There is, of course, a sense in which that is true. But there are also some important senses in which that is not true.[4] To look at such a motto day after day and to make the conventional, shallow misapplication of the profound truth it was meant to express is a sure way to disillusionment and despair when the day of testing comes.) To the young lady who wrote to me, "I can do all things" had become a religious *cliché*, a sentence taken out of context, a shallow slogan; and when in the day of testing she found the slogan didn't work, she was plunged into despair. It is one of the tragedies of our day that Scriptural words and phrases are being peddled like charms to an unsuspecting public, which is doomed to bitter disillusionment when the inevitable day of crisis comes.

The gloriously comforting fact for you and me, Mark, is that in the very important sense in which Paul was speaking, you and I *can* do all things through Christ, who strengthens us. No matter what the situation, be it poverty or wealth, sickness or health, success or failure, gladness or sorrow, honor or humiliation, we will find His omnipotent power sustaining us and leading us on toward final triumph.

In one of my former letters I quoted Paul's great paean of praise and triumph, which is found in the eighth chapter of his Letter to the Romans. Since, in a sense, this almost poetic outburst of confidence and assurance is but an expansion of his assertion "I can do all things," let me repeat it for you tonight.

"Who shall separate us from the love of Christ?" he asks. "Shall tribulation, or distress, or persecution, or famine, or nakedness, or peril, or sword? As it is written,

'For Thy sake we are being killed all the day long;
we are regarded as sheep to be slaughtered.'

[4] 2 Corinthians 12:7-10

"No, in all these things we are more than conquerors *through Him who loved us*. For I am sure that neither death nor life, nor angels, nor principalities, nor things present, nor things to come, nor powers, nor height, nor depth, nor anything else in all creation will be able to separate us from the love of God in Christ Jesus, our Lord." [5]

Hold on to that assurance, Mark. No matter what your present situation, no matter how great the odds against you, no matter how strewn your path may seem to be with failure and defeat, in God's eyes you are "more than a conqueror" through Him who loved you. With that assurance in your heart, you can pick yourself up, no matter how painful the defeat, and walk courageously onward toward the day of final victory.

John

[5] Romans 8:35-39

"I know that, as a believer, I should not fear death but, frankly, I cannot shake off the dread of dying. . . . Is it really true that a Christian is not afraid of death?"

XXIII · Open House in Heaven

Dear Mark:

As we grow in Christian faith and knowledge and gradually come closer to spiritual maturity, we become increasingly aware that there are some questions about the Christian life which cannot be answered with a simple yes or no. Suppose, for instance, that someone were to ask you: "Does a Christian like to sin?" How would you answer him? Perhaps if you were forced into an immediate reply, you would stammer either an uncertain yes or an uncertain no. The fact is that either answer could be right, *depending!* There is a sense in which a Christian likes to sin, and there is a sense in which he loathes it.

In this connection, let me remind you once again of that devastatingly crushing, yet marvelously comforting seventh chapter of Paul's Letter to the Romans. (Since both the King James and the Revised Standard Version of this chapter are very difficult to read, may I suggest that you read it in J. B. Phillips' paraphrase.) This is the chapter, you will recall, in which St. Paul admits, to his great dismay, that even after being a Christian for twenty years or more he still finds within himself *two* natures which are diametrically opposed to each other. According to his old nature, the one which he received at birth, he still delights in sin. According to his new nature, the one which he received when Jesus Christ took over his heart, he abominates the very thought of sinning. These two natures, he says, are at constant war within him. Sometimes the one gains the upper hand, sometimes the other, with the agonizing result that he exclaims at the end of this chapter "Wretched man that I am!" [1] In view of this, how do you suppose St. Paul would have answered the question, "Does a Christian like to sin?" In all probability he would have answered yes and no. According to his old nature, *yes*. According to his new nature, *no*.

I'm sure you see why I used the above approach for my answer to your question: "Is it really true that a Christian is not afraid to die?" I fear that there has been a lot of sentimental talk on this subject, talk which largely overlooks the contradiction which lives in every Christian heart. Believe me, there is a sense in which even the best of Christians are strangely uncomfortable and ill at ease at the very thought of death. Before the echo of that statement dies, however, let me be quick to add, there is also a sense in which the Christian looks forward to death as to a bright and welcome angel. Both are true. And both can be true of the same person. Each of us, no matter how far he has advanced in faith and knowledge, still carries within himself the inevitable weakness of the flesh as well as the strengthening and sustaining power of the Spirit.

Personally, I believe that it is not at all abnormal for any thinking adult to experience momentary fear at the thought of death, even though he be a believer. You and I are still playing host to a treacherous traitor in our bosom. We are by no means free from his subtle and sly suggestions. The same cunning voice which instilled doubt and fear into the hearts of our first parents will do its utmost to rob us of the confidence which God has given us in Christ. We must expect that.

Surely there is much about death that fills us with misgiving. The mystery of it. The pain of it. The finality of it. Its once-ness. Its loneliness — rather, its alone-ness, for each of us must tread

[1] Romans 7:24

its path alone. The inevitable separation from loved ones. The dark veil beyond which no human eye has ever seen and beyond which even the eye of faith can see only that which God in His love and wisdom has chosen to reveal. These are stark realities with which every thinking person must reckon. And in view of them I would be the last to romanticize or to sentimentalize the moment of physical death.

Indeed, there is much in the Bible that speaks against any romantic or sentimental view of death. The Bible calls death our "enemy." [2] Death was not a part of the divine plan for man. It entered into the human drama as the result of sin. God said to our first parents: "In the day that you eat of it you shall die." [3] That is, you shall become subject to death. Paul leaves no room for doubt about this. "Sin came into the world through one man," he says, "and *death through sin,* and so death spread to all men because all men sinned." [4] A materialistic society may look upon death as the inevitable result of purely natural processes. The believer looks upon death as the result of man's spiritual alienation from his Maker. "The wages of *sin* is death." [5]

It is impossible, therefore, to laugh death off as a mere accident or a mere incident in human life. It is the scourge of divine justice which has fallen upon a rebellious race. And even the believer, in those moments when the flesh gains the ascendancy over the spirit, may very well recoil from the prospect of meeting the final "enemy." [6] Remember, I am not saying that the believer *need* recoil from the thought of death. I am merely saying that, in his human weakness, he very well *may.* And if he does, he need not look upon these moments of fear and dread as evidence that his faith has died. They are merely evidences of the continuing struggle from which we shall finally be freed — only by the "angel of death" whose approach fills our heart with such mixed emotions.

The important thing for you and me to remember, Mark, is that God *did* something about this final enemy of which mortal man is so terribly afraid. In fact, that is precisely why

[2] 1 Corinthians 15:26   [3] Genesis 2:17
[4] Romans 5:12   [5] Romans 6:23
[6] 1 Corinthians 15:26

He sent His Son into the world. Let me refer briefly to two significant statements of Scripture in this connection. In the Letter to the Hebrews we read: "Since then the children [meaning the whole human family] have a common physical nature as human beings, He [Christ] also became a human being, so that by going through death as a man He might destroy him who had the power of death, that is, the devil; and might also set free those who lived their whole lives a prey to the fear of death." [7] And the other statement is this, taken from Paul's Second Letter to Timothy: "Christ has completely abolished death, and has now, through the Gospel, opened to us men the shining possibilities of the life that is eternal." [8]

What did the Bible writers mean by these two statements? You, of course, know the answer as well as I. They made these assertions within the framework of the total message which the Bible presents to us. Let's review that message briefly. Along with the rest of Scripture, Paul and the writer of Hebrews believed and taught that God had created the human family pure and sinless, fit for intimate daily fellowship with Him. But Satan, the prince of the fallen angels, ruined this relationship when he incited man to rebel against his Maker.[9] As a result of man's rebellion he came under "the rule of death," the inevitable consequence of sin. (The Bible speaks of death under three aspects — *physical* death, the cessation of physical life; *spiritual* death, the natural state of man prior to his rebirth by the Holy Spirit of God; and *eternal* death, the everlasting separation of man from his Maker.)

Now, the New Testament epistles tell us that Christ came into the world to *do* something about this intolerable human dilemma. By His sinless life as humanity's Substitute, by His perfect atonement for the total heap of human sin, and by His victorious resurrection from the dead on Easter morning, Christ vanquished the power of Satan and forever removed the blot of sin from the human soul. Sin, the root cause of man's fear of death, had been atoned for; and Satan, who had held the whiplash in his hand, had been robbed of his scourge. In the

[7] Hebrews 2:14, 15 P   [8] 2 Timothy 1:10 P
[9] Genesis 3:1-19

words of the Letter to the Hebrews, Christ had destroyed "him who had the power of death, that is, the devil," and had set free "those who lived their whole lives a prey to the fear of death."

We must remember that it was sin that gave death its hideous aspect and that it is *still* sin that makes death the frightening specter it is to many people today. The man who continues to live his life in a state of alienation from his Maker, who continues to live in open and admitted defiance of His laws, who consciously or unconsciously carries a burden of unforgiven sin upon his soul, may well look forward to death with fear and trembling. For that man death, according to Scripture, is a fearful moment, for he will have to stand, unreconciled and unforgiven, in the presence of a righteous God. But that man is not *you!* Through Christ you have been reconciled to your Father in heaven. Through Christ the burden of your guilt has been lifted. Through Christ your entire record of sin has been "washed away," "blotted out," "canceled." There is nothing in the heavenly record which should cause you to fear the moment of death, the moment when you step into the presence of the Father. With the problem of sin solved for you once and forever by the redeeming love of Christ, death need hold no terror for you.

Do you remember that gloriously triumphant passage with which Paul brings his wonderful fifteenth chapter of First Corinthians to a climax? He had devoted this entire chapter to a discussion of death and resurrection, pointing out again and again how the Christian's view of death must always take its perspective from Good Friday's cross and from Easter's empty tomb. Finally, when he reaches the high point of his presentation, he becomes eloquent and exclaims:

> " 'O death, where is thy victory?
> O death, where is thy sting?'

"The sting of death is sin, and the power of sin is the Law. But thanks be to God, who gives us the victory through our Lord Jesus Christ." [10] To Paul, death was a conquered enemy!

[10] 1 Corinthians 15:55, 56

His Champion — and ours — had met it and overcome it. And He had overcome it, first by removing its deadly sting, that is, by atoning for the sin of all mankind and thus rendering death harmless. And then also by rising from His own grave on Easter morning and becoming "the First Fruits of those who have fallen asleep." [11] The Christian need not be afraid of death because Christ, his Lord, has proved Himself death's Victor. And Christ, his Lord, has promised to share His victory with all who put their trust in Him. "Because I live, you will live also," He says.[12]

I realize, Mark, that much of what I have said so far tonight has been quite "technical." I see that, without having intended to, I have lapsed into the approach of a systematic theologian. I make no apologies for that. The fear of death can be banished only by an intelligent faith, and an intelligent faith will want to know on what it is based. I know you would not want to rest your faith on any sentimental vaporings. The other day in Los Angeles I saw a large billboard advertising a well-known cemetery. It pictured a graceful swan floating majestically on the surface of a glasslike pond. The legend, inscribed in elegant letters, read simply: "Beauty that Comforts." You know as well as I that death calls for more than beauty for its comfort! It calls for a Word of God, and that is what I have given you in my previous paragraphs.

Let me, however, proceed to a somewhat different approach to the problem which confronts you. I shall not deal in abstract doctrinal propositions, but I shall take you directly to the feet of Christ for an answer to the thoughts which trouble you. Come with me then to the night before our Savior died, and let us take our seats with the faithful few and listen to our Lord as He speaks with measured tones to those He loved:

"Let not your heart be troubled," He says. "Ye believe in God, believe also in Me. In My Father's house are many mansions. If it were not so, I would have told you. I go to prepare a place for you. And if I go and prepare a place for you, I will come again and receive you unto Myself, that where I am, there

[11] 1 Corinthians 15:20   [12] John 14:19

ye may be also." [13] I propose to take this wonderfully comforting farewell address of our Lord, phrase by phrase, and to share with you the spiritual insights which it reveals — insights which should bring fresh courage to your heart. Remember, it is your LORD who is speaking:

"Let not your heart be troubled." In all of your anxieties, fears, and misgivings — but especially in the particular fear about which we are talking tonight, the fear of death — I would suggest that you cultivate what some have called "the practice of the Savior's presence." For let there be no doubt about it; He *is* present with you every moment of the day. He has promised you that, and His Word cannot be broken.[14] Know that He is right there with you now! And in His omniscience He knows exactly what is on your heart. See Him and hear Him as He (as it were) puts His omnipotent arm around you and says in tones of quiet assurance: "Let not your heart be troubled." He who knows what is in the heart of man [15] knows the anxieties and fears to which all human flesh is heir. And He knows *your* doubts and *your* misgivings. It is the all-knowing Christ, the all-availing Savior, who is constantly at your side and who says to you, even as He said it to his depressed and despondent disciples on the night before His crucifixion: "Let not your heart be troubled." Draw fresh courage from those words with each new day, for He who spoke them was not a puny human as you and I, but the eternal and omnipotent Son of God Himself!

"Ye believe in God, believe also in Me." There is a vast difference, Mark, between merely believing in God and believing in the redeeming Son whom He has sent. Merely believing in God can provide very little comfort in the crisis hours of life, especially in that crisis hour which lies at the very end of our earthly journey. At that hour we shall want to hear the voice of "the Word of God Incarnate" saying: "Believe also in *ME!*" Christ is the Revelation of all those attributes of God which our heart yearns to know and which we have no other way of knowing.[16] It is He who has assured us of the Father's love. It is He who, by his vicarious life, death, and resurrection, has

13 John 14:1-3 KJ   14 Matthew 28:20

15 John 2:25   16 John 1:14-18

removed from our souls the stain of sin and made us fit for the company of His Father. It is He who has conquered death and who has promised to share His victory with us. It is He who, speaking with the authority of His divine Sonship, said: "I am the Resurrection and the Life; he who believes in Me, though he die, yet shall he live; and whoever lives and believes in Me shall never die." [17] In hours of doubt or fear or trial, especially during those hours when you contemplate the prospect of your journey's end, put your faith in Him! Not in a god in general, but in a God who has revealed His heart to you through His beloved Son. How important, when our feet seem ready to slip, that we hear His voice again and again: "Ye believe in God, believe also in *ME!*"

"In My Father's House are many mansions." There is music in those words, and sublimest poetry. Christ knew very well that there was something about the life beyond the grave which filled the hearts, even of the faithful, with dreadful awe and solemn wonder. He knew that even the thought of heaven could be frightening to weak and sinful mortals. And so He chooses His words carefully. He speaks fondly of His "Father's house." How wonderfully all our fears, all our misgivings are silenced by the tender associations of that picture! Our minds go back to our *earthly* father's house — with its sweet security, its freedom from responsibility, its complete assurance of constant love and care and safe protection. And then our minds go forward, carrying with them these same associations, only on an unspeakably higher level, to the Father's house which Christ assures us is just beyond the journey's end. There, too, sweet security shall be ours in the constant company of the Father, the Father who sent His Son to earth to bring His wandering children home.

In our Father's house are *"many mansions."* The Savior had a specific purpose for saying this. As His omniscient eye looked out across the centuries and saw all the countless throngs who would be brought to faith in Him, He thought it fitting to assure us that the expanse of His Father's house is limitless. There will be room for all who come to the Father through faith in Him. In fact, He is saying that there will be ample room for

[17] John 11:25

you, Mark. He who has singled you out as an object of His redeeming love and has promised to preserve you until the day of His heavenly kingdom,[18] He has made provisions for you in the mansions of the Father. I know that this language seems strange in a day when man-made satellites are circling the earth and men are talking of interplanetary travel. But let's remember that Christ had a penchant for expressing spiritual truths in picture language. In brief, what He is saying is: Don't let your heart be troubled; in the presence of My Father, whence I have come and whither I am going, there is room aplenty for you and all of My redeemed.

"If it were not so, I would have told you." I have always felt that there was something extremely remarkable about this and similar statements of the Savior. He consistently speaks about heaven with the certainty and the authority of one who had been there! As one who stands on a mountaintop, looking down into the valley beyond and telling his comrades behind him what he sees, so the Savior tells us about His Father's house — and ours. The streets of the eternal city are familiar to Him, the mansions of the Father's house stand clear and bright before His eyes. He *knows* what lies beyond the valley, for He has *come* from there. And so He can speak with an assurance which, on the lips of any other, would be nothing short of blasphemous presumption: "If it were not so, I would have told you." It is that kind of Savior you and I have. Surely, in matters of death and immortality and heaven, we can stake our souls on Him.

> My knowledge of that life is small,
> The eye of faith is dim;
> But 'tis enough that Christ knows all;
> And I shall be with Him.

"I go to prepare a place for you." Remember, these words were spoken on the eve of the Savior's crucifixion. Less than twenty-four hours later loving hands would lay His lifeless body into a tomb.[19] Some six weeks later the faithful would see His resurrected body ascend visibly from earth toward heaven.[20] Under the very shadow of these dramatic events which were

---

[18] 2 Timothy 4:18   [19] John 19:38-42   [20] Acts 1:9-11

crowding in upon Him He says: "I go to prepare a place for you." What did He mean? We may not be able to picture all that is meant by these simple and transparent words, but this we do know: His going ahead to the Father's house above was definitely for *our* benefit — "a place for *you*." His present activity in the heavenly mansions, His intercession before the Father's throne,[21] His sovereign rule [22] over heaven and earth,[23] and His loving care for those who have come to God by Him [24] — all are a preparation for our eternal joy and glory. Admittedly there is much that is left unexplained, much that our human reason would like to know but which at present is left unrevealed behind the veil; but we have been given the comforting and strengthening assurance that our elder Brother, Christ, has gone ahead and is "preparing a place" for us in the celestial mansions. Whatever that may mean in terms of precise detail, we can safely leave to Him. We know that He spoke these words for our reassurance. It is of our resurrected and ascended Christ that you and I sing:

> He lives, and grants me daily breath;
> He lives, and I shall conquer death;
> He lives my mansion to prepare;
> He lives to bring me safely there.

"And if I go . . . I will come again." Get the picture! Christ is taking leave of His despondent and distressed disciples. It is their last night together before He would be delivered into the hands of His enemies. As a mother soothes her weeping child, from whom she must be separated for a moment, with the whisper of assurance, "I will come again," so the Savior tries to soothe the fears of His loved ones with the certain prospect of His imminent return. I must leave you now, He says, but — "let not your heart be troubled. . . . I will come again!" And how effectively that simple promise, that certain prospect, poured courage into their fainting hearts is amply demonstrated by the Bible record. Trials and afflictions, pains and persecutions, "frightings and fears within and without" — all would have to be borne, to be sure. But only until *HE* would come again, and then all would be supremely well. His promised coming, either at the

---

[21] Hebrews 7:25   [22] 1 Peter 3:22
[23] Ephesians 1:21, 22   [24] John 10:9-16

death of the world or at the death of the believer, cast a golden glow over all the road that stretched ahead. They were walking toward the light of His return. In that light all shadows fell behind them. In that light they found the courage to walk courageously onward — straight to their journey's end.

So, too, with us. All sorrows, all heartaches, all disappointments and bereavements, all fears of what may lie in store for us as we approach the journey's end — all lose their sting and bitterness in the sweetness of the Savior's promise: "I will come again." I will come again to turn your sorrows into joy, your heartaches into gladness, your doubts and fears into unshakable assurance, your separations and bereavements into heavenly reunions in My Father's house above. I will come again to lead you across the threshold, out of darkness into light, into the eternal mansions of My Father, prepared for you and for all who love Him.

"I will come again *and receive you unto Myself, that where I am, there ye may be also.*" As we trace the trend of the Savior's thoughts during the closing scenes of His earthly life, we are impressed by one compelling force which lay behind His every word and deed: His affectionate attachment to His faithful few and His deep desire that His intimate and free companionship with them be continued in His Father's house above. Thus, for instance, in His great prayer of intercession later that same night, after imploring His Father's blessing upon all believers of all time, He climaxes His prayer with this jewel of all petitions: "Father, I want those whom You have given Me to be with Me where I am; I want them to see that glory which You have made Mine — for You loved Me before the world began." [25] He shares with His Father a desire which, when He repeats it to His believers, becomes a promise: "I will come again and receive you unto Myself, that where I am, there ye may be also." It is not putting it too simply to say that Christ has secured His Father's approval and permission to bring His friends along with Him into His Father's house. By His redeeming act, by His vicarious life, death, and resurrection, of which I have written at great length in some of my previous letters, He has unlocked

[25] John 17:24 P

the door of His Father's home to all who will come in humble penitence and faith. Heaven is now an open house! Christ is standing at the threshold ready to receive us. "Where I am, there ye may be also."

I have given you these opening words of the Savior's farewell address to His disciples phrase by phrase. Now let's put them back together and let them speak directly to your heart — and mine. For they are addressed to *our* hearts just as surely as they were addressed to those in the upper room that night. "Let not your heart be troubled," the Savior says. "Ye believe in God, believe also in Me. In My Father's house are many mansions. If it were not so, I would have told you. I go to prepare a place for you. And if I go and prepare a place for you, I will come again and receive you unto Myself, that where I am, there ye may be also." The One who spoke those words was none other than the eternal, pre-existent Son of God, who came down from heaven to redeem your soul so that you could live with Him forever in the glorious life which follows death. Believe Him. Trust Him. Stake all your hope on Him.

> Upon a life I did not live,
> Upon a death I did not die,
> Another's life, another's death,
> I stake my whole eternity.

Don't put your trust in anyone or anything less! I know that the world is full of lesser assurances, but I know, too, that these lesser assurances do not sustain the anxious heart in the major crises of life, particularly in the hour of death. Men of all ages have sought for pledges of immortality, for proofs of a happy life beyond the grave. In our day it has become the fashion to point, for instance, to the dying leaves of autumn and to the tender shoots of springtime as pictures of human death and resurrection — and as pledges of a life beyond the tomb. But when the cold finger of icy death comes tapping at our shoulder, there will be no comfort in the fact that October is the time of falling leaves and that springtime is the season when the lilacs and the lilies bloom. At that moment nothing less will comfort our turbulent souls than the vision of the Savior, triumphant in the skies, with the seal of victory over death in

His nail-pierced hands and the shout of assurance on His lips: "Because I live, you will live also!" [26]

His victory over the grave is our pledge of life eternal. His empty tomb proclaims to us that our grave, too, shall someday be empty. The Scriptures tell us: "Christ has been raised from the dead, the First Fruits of those who have fallen asleep." [27] Just as the "first fruits" are the forepledge, the foretaste, of a later and more general harvest, so Christ's resurrection is the guarantee and forepledge of *our* resurrection to life eternal in that later, greater harvest. For you and me, Mark, death need hold no terror. Our Savior has lifted the veiling cloud which hung heavily over what seemed to be our journey's end, and at the end of the road that winds up the far side of the valley we see the warm and shining lights of our Father's house. Because of the atonement and intercession of our Savior, the door is open and the welcome mat is out. Once across the threshold, we shall be "forever with the Lord." [28]

> "Forever with the Lord!"
> Amen! So let it be,
> Life from the dead is in that word,
> 'Tis immortality.

To this Lord, who has redeemed you, body and soul, for time and for eternity, you can safely entrust your ultimate destiny — today, tomorrow, and forever.

John

[26] John 14:19   [27] 1 Corinthians 15:20
[28] 1 Thessalonians 4:17